How
FIND ME
Lost Me

A Breach of Trust Told by the Psychic
Who Didn't See It Coming.

DAN BALDWIN

A Do as I Say Not as I Did Book for Writers

ISBN-13: 978-1547044078
ISBN-10: 1547044071

CONTENTS

*The documentation in the Appendix isn't presented in chronological order. Often a single e-mail will refer to more than one topic. Refer to the Appendix number as you read the book to follow the events.

"A verbal contract isn't worth the paper it's written on."

~Attributed to movie mogul Samuel Goldwyn

Author's Preface
Do As I Say Not As I Did

Of all the books I have co-authored or ghostwritten the one I knew, absolutely knew beyond a shadow of a doubt, that I wouldn't need a written contract, letter of agreement, or even a confirming e-mail for was the one I began with Kelly Snyder in 2009.

Writers beware. Regardless of how well you know someone, the depth of experience you have with someone, or how much you trust someone, if you plan on writing something together – insist on a clear, concise and written contract.

Do as I say not as I did.

This isn't a book on contract law. It is a warning of what can happen when a writer ignores his or her basic responsibility to consider the potential legal ramifications of relying on someone's spoken word vs. the strength of the written word. How *Find Me II* by Dan Baldwin and Kelly Snyder became *They Are Not Yet Lost* by Dan Baldwin is an interesting and cautionary tale. The story begins somewhere near the middle in which I was dismissed from a group of volunteer psychic investigators, a group and a cause in which I had invested nearly 15 years of my life. The reason for removal was for violating a code of ethics by stating a fact long-recognized by the organization. That's right. Removal from membership was based on saying something that appeared on the Find Me official website and in books and other materials – more on that and how it is related to co-authoring a book follows.

The officers and board of directors cited two reasons for removal. The second was the previously mentioned book. Each issue is reviewed here with extensive documentation because the officers and board of directors married the two. As you read, keep firmly in mind the words of wisdom attributed to movie mogul Samuel Goldwyn. "A verbal contract isn't worth the paper it's written on."

*The obligatory disclaimer: I am not an attorney and this book does not offer legal advice.

CHAPTER ONE

Killing One Bird with Two Stones

The issues covered in this work are: my removal as a member, board of directors member, and as president of the board of directors; and the twisting path that led to my book about psychic detecting cases handled by the Find Me group. To avoid confusion each is discussed briefly in this and the following chapter so the reader can keep matters in perspective. Although the focus is on the book, both issues must be addressed. Again, the officers and board of directors married the two issues.

I had written an "as told to" book titled *Find Me* published in 2007. The book related the story of a group of volunteer psychics organized by Kelly Snyder to find missing persons and solve crimes. I was there from the beginning and served as a board member and President of the Board from the time the group became a 501c3 Corporation (IRS) until 2015. As a pendulum dowser I worked almost every case during that time frame. Also, I volunteered with the group's search and rescue sister organization, Arizona Search Track and Rescue (AZSTAR) as a "groundpounder" during on-site investigations in California, Colorado and throughout Arizona. As with the other members of the organization, my work was as an unpaid volunteer.

Imagine my astonishment when I received an e-mail stating the officers and board of directors had removed me from the organization.

"You have been removed from Find Me as a Board member and regular member. The board decided that you violated all five of the Code of Ethics by your statement that you are a co-founder of Find Me." (Appendix 1)

The full membership was notified of the board's action by e-mail on September 27, 2015.

"Member Dan Baldwin was removed from the FM Group and Board of Directors for violating the code of ethics." (Appendix 2)

No explanation or description of that violation was provided. No notice was made that the decision was made at a special board meeting held months earlier.

Although I was President of the Board of Directors at that time I was not notified of the board meeting and was therefore prohibited from providing what I consider significant information regarding the issues. Find Me is an Arizona non-profit corporation falling under the federal 501c3 section of the internal revenue code. The board's action in not notifying a board member of such a meeting violates the Find Me Bylaws.

4.06 Removal of Directors
(b) for cause or no cause, if before any meeting of the board at which a vote on removal will be made the director in question is given electronic or written notification of the board's intention to discuss her/his case and is given the opportunity to be heard at a meeting of the board.

A board member can be removed for any cause or no cause at all. There is no need to fabricate a cause for action. In a removal, however, that board member must be notified of the meeting and be given the opportunity to be heard at that meeting. Again, although I was President of the Board of Directors at that time I was not notified of the meeting and therefor prohibited from attending and being heard – an action in direct violation of the group's 501c3 (IRS) bylaws.

True Confessions. I participated in a similar removal of two board members some time earlier. As a board member I should have known or at least looked up the proper procedure and insisted that it be followed. I did not. As they say, "my bad." They also say, "Two wrongs don't make a right" or, in this case three wrongs don't make a right. What should be noted is that the removal of board members in violation of the Find Me bylaws isn't a one-time occurrence. Rather, it is a pattern of corporate behavior by the officers and board of directors. (Appendix 3)

*I did not vote for removal in those votes, stating that the length of service and commitment of the members in question outweighed any infraction of the code of ethics.

CHAPTER TWO

The Undiscussed Reason

Find Me II – The Casebook was also an issue, but, according to emails from Snyder, one that was not discussed at the board meeting.

"The Find Me Book is also at issue here, but may lead into legal action, so it was left out of the equation for determining you being removed....Your stance on the fact that you believe you can publish a book about Find Me is another board issue but has to do with our legal stance on how we will address your actions. If you proceed with the book without my consent then it is something the courts will ultimately decide."

(Appendix 4 – E-mail Kelly Snyder to Dan Baldwin and Find Me Board July 16, 2015)

"I am not all that sensitive, but this issue and the book issue made it seem almost like a hostile takeover and that would affect me with Denise and other "business" and personal related items in play…

(Appendix 5 – E-mail Snyder to Baldwin July 8, 2015 – grammar/spelling in the original)

"They knew nothing about the book issue and made their decision based on your untruthfulness.. this divagation won't work Dan, since this chapter hasn't been written yet… we are waiting for your next move. ..!"

(Appendix 6 – E-mail from Kelly Snyder to Dan Baldwin, July 17, 2015) grammar/spelling in the original)

What does the reader learn from this? The removal involved two issues and one of them was either kept from the officers and board of directors or not considered by them. These two issues will be developed in the following chapters. The dismissal issue will be addressed first and for two reasons: to avoid confusing the reader when the documentation refers at times to both issues and because the officers and board linked the two issues.

CHAPTER THREE

What Makes a Co-Founder?

Whether or not *Find Me II – The Casebook* (a working title) was kept from the board or just ignored by them, at some point the officers and board of directors linked the two issues. The two issues are key to a letter from the Find Me attorney covered in later chapters. Snyder e-mailed on July 6, 2015. "…You have been telling people and recently put into print on your book stating you are a co-founder of Find Me. You are not a co-founder. You are a (sic) inaugural member and board member. That would be an accurate and appropriate statement I am happy to support."

July 8, 2015: "For the record…. I have only heard you make that reference in recent months … it bothered me then, but really only mattered when you started putting it in print." (grammar/spelling in the original). That is an interesting statement because the term co-founder or founder in reference to me had been in print multiple times since 2007. (Appendix 7)

Two points should be understood at the beginning of this chapter. One, I had been using the term co-founder of Find Me publicly and in the presence of Find Me members, board members and officers for years. The term "co-founder" or "founder" had been used in print and electronic media in reference to me by the Find Me organization from at least as early as 2007. Two, once I was made aware that the term was a matter of concern I immediately agreed to the use of another term. "Co-founder" appeared on the back cover of my book on dowsing, *The Practical Pendulum*. I immediately changed the term to "inaugural member" on the ebook and paperback versions. Snyder even e-mailed thanking me for my understanding and professionalism. (Appendix 7).

I believed the issue had been amicably resolved at that point. As I e-mailed, the term was "no biggie" to me.

Snyder said he had heard me use the term only in recent months. Perhaps, but he surely had been reading the same term for nearly half a decade. Although the group had recognized me as a founder or co-founder for years, the removal proceeded anyway. Consider the following.

———

At the time of the removal, the Board of Directors biographies page on the official Find Me website stated, "President – Dan Baldwin. Dan Baldwin, whose skill is pendulum dowsing, is a founding member of Find Me and he has participated as a "ground pounder" on numerous search and rescue missions." (Appendix 8)

———

I asked an attorney the same question that heads this chapter. Gary A. Wolf, P.C. stated, "As to our client's co-founding status, the Arizona Corporation Commission's website shows our client as one of the founding board members not only in your client's 2011 Articles of Incorporation, but also in the 2012, 2013, 2014, and 2015 Annual Reports filed by your client. Your client's own website that he reviewed and approved showed at one time our client's founding board member status (please see enclosed screenshot), PR releases and book jackets that were reviewed and approved by your client showed our client as a founding member...."

Wolf wrote, "The incorporation documents filed with the Arizona Corporation Commission in 2011 that your client personally filed and executed reflects that Mr. Baldwin was in fact a founding Board member of FIND ME, which makes him a *"de facto"* founding member of FIND ME. As a founding Board member, Mr. Baldwin is free to represent this fact." (Appendix 9)

––––––––

The Articles of Incorporation of the Find Me organization are public records and are available for review online through the Arizona Corporation Commission website and can be reviewed at your convenience.

http://corporations.images.azcc.gov/03637757.pdf

http://ecorp.azcc.gov/Details/Corp?corpId= 17050874

––––––––

Find Me as Told to Dan Baldwin, a book about the founding and early members of the organization, was published in 2007. Chapter One, Finding Find Me, states on page 16, "...If you haven't guessed by now, this psychic was the same person working with Kelly to found what would become Find Me. Dan was asked to join, and he became the third member of the group." (Appendix 10)

––––––––

As Snyder noted in his quote on *The Practical Pendulum*, "Dan has been with Find Me since its inception in 2001." (Appendix 11)

––––––––

Find Me as Told to Dan Baldwin went into a second edition in 2012. The manuscript's reference to being the third member appears on page ten in this version.

More to the point, the back cover carries photos and brief bios of Dan Baldwin and Kelly Snyder beneath "The Authors" section. "Dan Baldwin... He is a founding member of Find Me who often participates in 'ground pounding' with the group's sister organization...." The term founding member appears only one inch above the beginning of Snyder's bio. (Appendix 12)

––––––––

In 2013 the promotion for an interview with Kelly Snyder and Dan Baldwin on *Supernatural Girlz Radio* carries a photo of the book and includes the line, "Kelley (sic) Snyder is a former law enforcement official who, along with Dan Baldwin created an all-volunteer panel of psychic mediums and active law enforcement." (Appendix 13)

––––––––

On June 19, 2015 I e-mailed a query letter for his review. The letter would be sent to agents/publishers regarding *Find Me II – The Casebook*. Paragraph four of that draft states, "Find Me was founded in 2002 by Kelly Snyder, a retired federal agent with more than 25 years of experience in the Drug Enforcement Agency. I am a co-founder of the group." (Appendix 14)

The terms founder and co-founder in reference to my participation on the organization had been in use since at least 2007 in Find Me books, in promotional materials, and in direct correspondence with Snyder. From 2007 into 2015 nothing was ever said to me about the use of the term co-founder. There were no complaints, no requests to refrain from using the term, no requests to use an alternative term.

What would have made something so old a new issue in 2015? It's just my opinion, but I believe the timeline, the comments, and the events relating to *Find Me II – The Casebook* indicated that the issue of that book is at the heart of the matter.

The board was notified of all the above in an effort to resolve the situation.

Again, the issue of removal from the board of directors and from the membership is included here because it was linked with the book issue by the board and officers. Additionally, the way the removal and the follow-up events were handled provides an insight into the thought processes and ethical standards of the parties involved.

––––––––

The question should be asked. Which is the greater violation of the Find Me Code of Ethics: a member making a statement long-recognized by the organization or the board of directors conducting a vote in violation of the bylaws of a 501c3 (IRS) corporation?

———

Lesson Learned: The consequences of not having a good contract can have surprising and unpleasant effects on other aspects of a writer's life.

CHAPTER FOUR

An Offer

The goal at that time was simply to right what I consider to have been a wrong – a belief supported by the facts documented here. An offer was made through a mediation service. My thoughts at the time were basic. I had been wronged by the actions of the officers and board of directors, a matter that had been made public. The goal was to have them right that wrong: reinstate me as a member in good standing as a member and board member and notify the membership and other involved parties. I offered to resign once that was done. At one point I even provided a sample resignation letter.

This process consumed some time, but is not relevant to the co-author issues in this book. A sample of the offers made is included in the appendix for the reader's reference. (Appendix 15)

CHAPTER FIVE
A Preview of Events

Because the issue not discussed, *Find Me II – The Casebook*, involves a number of elements, a brief outline of the information that appears in following chapters is appropriate – a roadmap to help keep the reader on a twisting and turning track. These, and other relevant matters, will be covered in detail.

2001 – Find Me founded. Baldwin is in at the inception and is recognized as the third member of the organization.

2007 – *Find Me as Told to Dan Baldwin* published. Page 16 notes that Baldwin "…was the same person working with Kelly to found what would become Find Me."

2009 – Baldwin approaches Snyder to write a follow up book and a 50/50 verbal agreement is made.

Baldwin begins writing *Find Me Two* (working title). The copyright notice reads "© Dan Baldwin/Kelly Snyder 2009"

The book becomes an on-and-off project for a number of years.

2015 – A first draft of the book, now identified with the working title *Find Me II – The Casebook* is completed.

February 21, 2015 – Snyder e-mails Baldwin regarding his, Snyder's, conversations with Cynthia Cannell of the Cannell Agency in New York.

Baldwin e-mails a rough draft version of *Find Me II – The Casebook* to Cynthia Cannell of the Cannell Agency in New York. Snyder is copied in on the e-mail, which also includes a copy of the manuscript. The title page notes the copyright of Dan Baldwin and Kelly Snyder.

April 12, 2014 – Snyder e-mails Baldwin that his agent

(Cannell) wants him to do the book in his own voice and that he is "doing my best to figure you into this equation."

April 13, 2015 – Baldwin reminds Snyder that the work is the property of Baldwin and Snyder and cannot be appropriated by either party. Snyder says he is deciding on which chapters to "select" for his book.

May 8, 2015 – referencing Snyder's agreement with his agent, Baldwin writes, "If the contract is for our book, I need to see a copy of it. If it's for the Kelly book, no need."

July 8, 2015 – Snyder thanks Baldwin for his "understanding and professionalism" in handling the "co-founder/inaugural member" issue.

Snyder states that he is having Baldwin's biography removed from the Find Me website. (Note: according to the timeline, the removal from the website occurred before the vote for removal.)

July 9, 2015 – Baldwin e-mails Snyder that *Find Me II – The Casebook* is ready for publication in paperback and as an e-book stating that their 50/50 agreement was in place and would be honored. The ready-for-print book lists Baldwin and Snyder as copyright owners.

July 14, 2015 – Snyder e-mails Baldwin that he has been removed from Find Me as a board member and President of the Board. Snyder demands to be disassociated with *Find Me II – The Casebook.*

July 17, 2015 – In a response to an e-mail from Baldwin, Snyder states of the book, "It's yours to keep, just make sure there are NO references that I have anything to do with it and that NONE of my comments are in the book."

July 29, 2017 – Baldwin receives a letter from an attorney representing Snyder and the Find Me board of directors and officers regarding *Find Me II – The Casebook.* The letter contains a number of inaccurate statements, including that Snyder independently wrote 17 chapters of the book, that Snyder provided copyrighted audio recordings, and that Baldwin had stated he,

Baldwin, would copyright the work in his own name.

Baldwin begins a series of attempts to mediate the situation, particularly the inaccurate statements made in the letter from the Find Me attorney.

November 2, 2015 – Baldwin, through an arbitrator, notifies Snyder and the Find Me board of directors and officers that he will publish the book, honoring Snyder's demand to be disassociated as an author or co-author.

November 3, 2015 – The Find Me attorney requests additional time for Snyder to review the manuscript. (Time was granted.)

November 25, 2015 – Baldwin notifies the Find Me organization attorney that if Snyder has no interest in arbitrating/mediating the matter then Baldwin will move forward with the book.

December 18, 2015 – Baldwin's arbitration counselor notifies the Find Me attorney that the lack of response indicates that all their concerns have been met and that he is moving forward with the manuscript.

There is no response from the attorney, Snyder or the Find Me Board of Directors and officers.

December, 2015 – *They Are Not Yet Lost* by Dan Baldwin is published in paperback and e-mail formats.

2016 – *They Are Not Yet Lost* wins first place in the New Age Division of the Arizona-New Mexico Book Awards Competition

———

It is interesting to note that although the terms "founder" and "co-founder" had been recognized by the Find Me organization since at least 2007, terms did not become an issue until July, 2015.

CHAPTER SIX

A Letter to the Board of Directors and Officers

Was the board of directors of Find Me ever made aware of the "issue not discussed?" Considering that possibility, an attempt to set the record straight was e-mailed to the officers and board of directors in the hope that the complete story would become part of the record.

————

Dan Baldwin

July 16, 2015

A statement for the board of directors of Find Me.

I was informed on July 14, 2015 that I was removed from the board of directors and the Find Me organization for using the term "co-founder" of Find Me. This action was taken without my knowledge – I was an active board member at that time – and I was not allowed to provide input into the decision making process. In the interest of fairness and basic courtesy, I ask that the following be entered into the minutes at the next Find Me board of directors meeting.

————

"On July 6, 2015 I was informed that my use of the term 'co-founder' of Find Me was an issue that needed to be corrected and that I could use the term 'inaugural member' instead. I had/have no problem with that change and I responded immediately to comply.

I have used the term 'co-founder' of Find Me in writing and verbally for more than a decade as a convenient way of describing my length of service with the organization. I attended the initial meetings of the group that became Find Me and have been a member since its inception.

I have used the term co-founder verbally at board meetings, presentations and events, particularly at the round-robin introductions at various meetings during those years.

I have used the term verbally in the presence of officers, board members, and the CEO/Founder.

The term was in print on the initial back cover of my 2015 book *The Practical Pendulum*. This has been changed.

The term was in my board member bio on our web site as of July, 2015.

The term 'founding member' of Find Me appears on the back cover of the as-told-to Find Me book *Find Me,* which has been in print for years.

As of July 15, the term co-founder was in use only on the back cover of my book and on the Find Me website.

When notified that this was a matter of concern and that my bio had been removed from the website, I immediately complied with the notice. I took steps to change the reference in *The Practical Pendulum* to 'inaugural member' as requested and that is in progress now with the production facilities.

On July 8, 2015 I received an e-mail from Kelly Snyder stating, "Thank you for handling this with understanding and professionalism."

I thought that was the end of the matter. The concern was stated and immediately addressed.

The next e-mail on the matter stated that I had been removed from the board and the membership for using the term co-founder.

During all the years in which I used the term co-founder no one ever protested, complained or asked me to refrain from its use. Had such a request been made, I would have complied immediately as I did in this situation.

Again, considering that the matter of my removal was taken without my knowledge and the board was not given what I consider important input into the decision making process, I request that this statement be entered into the minutes of the next board of directors meeting.

Dan Baldwin

July 16, 2016 (sic)

————

If any board member has any questions about this matter, I am available by phone or e-mail at any time.

Dan

————

The response to that request came in a July 17, 2017 e-mail from Snyder.

"They knew nothing about the book issue and made their decision based on your untruthfulness.. this divagation won't work Dan, since this chapter hasn't been written yet…we are waiting for your next move.
"Since you are providing this to the entire board it is NOT something that needs read in to the minutes and there is no precedence for it. You are a "VOLUNTEER"…. Not a paid employee..!!" (grammar/spelling in the original) (Appendix 6)

CHAPTER SEVEN

Origins of *Find Me II – The Casebook*

A writer working with a co-author must document everything every step of the way, including e-mail and other correspondence. If things go south you may find your co-author making false statements or is suffering from false memory about you and the project. For example, I initiated the *Find Me II* project in 2009. The book was to be a Dan Baldwin and Kelly Snyder project – not a Find Me organization sponsored project. This is important; the book was to be about Find Me but not a product of Find Me. The responsibilities were specific. Snyder would provide raw investigative files and personal input on the individual cases. I would write the book. It would be written what I call standard business style, the same style used in the *Find Me as Told to Dan Baldwin* book. (I was at the time and still am a full-time professional author, co-author and ghostwriter with more than 60 works to my credit.) The agreement was to a 50/50 split of ownership, profits and expenses. The agreement was also verbal. A contract should have been drafted and signed at that time.

Do as I say; not as I did.

On Monday, July 6, 2015 Snyder e-mailed:

"I decided in 2011 to write another book, but 100% in my style of writing. Later that year or in early 2012 you asked if I was considering writing another book. I stated at that time I was considering it, but again repeated that it was going to be in my style. You stated 'if you need or want my help I would be glad to help you.'

"With that said, I stated I would someday figure out the direction of the book. Co-authorship was never mentioned. You agreed to help me, but now I am getting the distinct impression you see yourself as co-author...."
(Appendix 16)

Later in an e-mail to me and the Board of Directors of Find Me, Snyder wrote," I have been granted rights to write a book about Find Me, but you have not. You are not a co-author as you are suggesting. You asked if you could assist me, but that verbal agreement was not authorizing you being a co-author. Is it just me or does there seem to be a pattern developing here...?" (grammar/spelling in the original) (Appendix 4, fifth paragraph)

Find Me II The Casebook (a working title sometimes also called *Find Me Two*) was a co-author project initiated by me in 2009. The first page typed out was the cover sheet which read:
> *Find Me II*
> *(Working Title)*
> © *Dan Baldwin/Kelly Snyder*
> (Appendix 17)

The book was begun two years before and well-underway by the time Snyder claims to have begun thinking about the project.

Although Snyder states the work began in 2011, he had contacted a literary agent recommended by a Find Me member on January 21, 2010. He e-mailed an early draft of the manuscript to Cynthia Cannell of the Cannell Literary Agency in New York. I e-mailed him that day that the book needed a grammar/spelling review and that there were holes that needed filling. He responded, "I filled them in and read the entire thing one more time." Also, note the use of "we" instead of "I" in. "Great talking to you . attached are chapters we have completed so far." (grammar/spelling in the original) (Appendix 18)

This is an example of the type of bizarre claims a writer can face without a contract with his co-author. Snyder here states that he has read and forwarded a manuscript that he later claims could not have existed for another year or more.

On October 27, 2010 I e-mailed Snyder about progress on the book.

"Do we have other similar cases where only volunteers from the group were involved? Anyway, send me notes on another chapter ASAP and let's push this thing on through as far as we can."   Earlier that day I had e-mailed a progress report noting that I was beginning to work on an eighth chapter. By October, 2010 the first draft was already one third complete. (Appendix 19)

Earlier in the day (October 27, 2010) he e-mailed me:

"I would suggest that we either do three or four cases like Sheddy in one chapter or NOT at all. I have zero on the case and it is not a case I assigned to the group."

And about half an hour earlier I had sent Snyder a complete manuscript as of that date.

"Kelly,

"Attached is the complete new manuscript with the Stover chapter added." Note in the e-mail that seven chapters have already been written by 2010 and that I am the writer of those chapters. (Appendix 19)

Falsehood or false memory?

Does it matter in a he said/she said matter.

Snyder's claims are shown to be just that – claims, and unsupportable claims at that – by his own words. In a he said/she said situation keeping records does matter. As far as Snyder initiating the work in 2011 or 2012, his own e-mail record shows he was already involved during 2010.

That's why documentation is so important. In the above situation one co-author is stating a demonstrable untruth. Presumably a co-author willing to write untruthful statements would be willing to verbalize those statements. Documenting your agreement and the back-and-forth that occurs during the project is essential.

CHAPTER EIGHT

A Matter of Style

The Find Me Board and officers, through their attorney, would later claim that Snyder wrote and owned the copyright to 17 chapters of *Find Me II – The Casebook,* which brings up an interesting subject since Snyder claims to have initiated a work "in my style of writing."

As stated previously, the style agreed on in 2009 was a standard business style, the same style used in *Find Me as Told to Dan Baldwin.* Nothing was said about writing the work in Snyder's style. That topic did not come up until after the manuscript had been sent to the New York agent.

The original version of the book had a Chapter 19 with the byline Kelly Snyder. (If the book was written by Snyder there would be no need for a byline on a single chapter.) He wrote a draft, which I rewrote for grammar, spelling and style. His draft ended with the following line:

I will most likely expand this or work on it a little more,
but feel free to add, delete or make it prettier....
(Appendix 20)

If the chapter was already in his style, there would be no need for a rewrite. Again, the matter of "his style" was not yet an issue.

An April 12, 2015 Snyder responded to an e-mail, "I am waiting for a response from Cynthia which should give me some direction... nothing has changed.... She wants me to do the book on my own and I am doing my best to figure you into this equation !!" (grammar/spelling in original) (Appendix 21)

The interesting thing, therefore is a question. If, as Snyder and the board and officers claim, initiated the book to be written in his style, why wasn't the book written in that style in the first place? Obviously, from Snyder's e-mail regarding his conversation with her, the book as presented was in another style. Writers do not send unfinished works to agents or publishers. That's a direct route to the trash bin.

Note two things regarding this time frame. The problem regarding the co-founder issue did not come up until after this date. Two, the problems regarding authorship, copyright and other matters discussed in following chapters did not come up until after this date.

CHAPTER NINE

Legal Matters

A writer who does not have a contract with his co-author may find himself unexpectedly walking on legal ground, territory filled with real and potential landmines. In this situation, legal action was threatened more than once. There was a threat worse than that. I earn my living as a writer. Although I have been published traditionally, most of my works are published through Amazon and its sister organization CreateSpace, which distribute to other outlets.

The final paragraph in the July 14, 2015 e-mail from Snyder stated, "My new attorney Maria Crimi Speth will be sending you a confirmation of this request and details surrounding this request. Any reference that you are a co-founder of Find Me on Amazon also needs to be removed. *My attorney will also be including Amazon in on our correspondence.*" (emphasis mine) (Appendix 1)

This strikes right at the heart of my livelihood and was something that had to be addressed. Attempts to do so directly, through a mediation service, and through an attorney failed, which required a response to get the facts of the story out in a public venue – this book. So, this book serves a double purpose: letting the documentation set the record straight on bogus claims about me and my work and to serve as a cautionary tale to writers foolish enough – like me – to trust spoken words over written ones.

Legal action or at least the threat of legal action is something a writer may face. Again, to avoid he said/she said situations it is essential that the writer keep copies of all correspondence and documentation related to the project. Win or lose, legal action is costly and time consuming. Having documentation in hand can short-circuit that process. Legal action was repeatedly threatened in this situation.

A July 16, 2015 e-mail from Snyder stated that Find Me was trademarked and that I was not authorized to use the name for *Find Me II – The Casebook.* "Use of this name will be immediate grounds for legal action."

"The Find Me Book is also at issue here, but may lead into legal action, so it was left out of the equation for determining you being removed... Your stance on the fact that you believe you can publish a book about Find Me is another board issue, but has to do with our legal stance on how we will address your actions. If you proceed with the book without my consent then it is something the courts will ultimately decide..."

"Also be advised that Denise Goodwin-Pace has notified her attorneys about this book issue with you, since you have also signed a 'shopping agreement w with her (Article 4.1) that does not allow you to say or do anything without her express permission..."

A July 29, 2015 letter from the legal firm of Jarburg/Wilk stated, "This firm represents Kelly Snyder and Find Me, Inc. in connection with the protection and enforcement of their intellectual property rights...."

At some point the board of directors decided to inject itself into the situation between Baldwin and Snyder. *Find Me II – The Casebook* was about the Find Me organization, but it was never a product of that organization. It was always a Baldwin/Snyder production. Why the officers and Board of Directors of Find Me decided to get involved in the matter is a mystery. The officers and board of directors in 2015 were: Kelly Snyder, Sunny Dawn Johnson, Dave Campbell, John DenBoer, Peggy Rometo, Scott Snyder, and Dan Baldwin. (After my removal, my position was filled by Scott Snyder.)

No legal action followed these threats.

And when I offered the opportunity to resolve specific matters relating to the book in a legally binding environment the officers and board of directors did not respond.

CHAPTER TEN
Enter AZSTAR

Arizona Search Track and Rescue (AZSTAR) is a sister group to Find Me. I have been a "groundpounder" volunteer on numerous searches with that group from California to Colorado. For some reason AZSTAR injected itself into the "issue not discussed" matter.

Mr. Baldwin:

You are in possession of written information, pictures and other data, including but not limited to, a chapter for a book that was provided to Kelly Snyder of Find Me for inclusion in the book being authored by Kelly Snyder about Find Me and the work that the organization does.

Arizona Search Track and Rescue, Inc. (AZ STaR) does not now nor has ever conveyed to Dan Baldwin permission to utilize this information (pictures, emails, written word or any other data) and furthermore Arizona Search Track and Rescue does not convey in any way shape or form, any permissions to Dan Baldwin to utilize any information (pictures, emails, written word or any other data) about AZ STaR and/or any information relative to any search & rescue missions that Arizona Search Track and Rescue, Inc. has been involved with.

Should you have any questions regarding this request, please direct it to:

Gregory Robinson,
Attorney at Law
Farley, Robinson, & Larsen

6040 N. Seventh Street
Suite #300
Phoenix, AZ 85014-1803
Sincerely,
Kristi Smith
President
Arizona Search Track and Rescue, Inc.
Cc: Kelly Snider, Find Me
      Denise Goodwin Pace, Looking Up Productions
(Appendix 22)

———————

Kristi Smith, President of AZSTAR, had written a chapter for *Find Me II – The Casebook* about working with a search and rescue organization. At her request (see above) this chapter was pulled from the final version. She was informed that no proprietary information, documents or photographs were part of the book. The letter illustrates the kind of nonsense a writer in a co-author situation sometimes faces. Neither AZSTAR nor Find Me nor any other person or organization can declare themselves exempt from comment. Neither organization had a right to censorship.

Notice that the letter was copied to Denise Goodwin Pace of Looking Up Productions. What had begun as a simple matter between two men had escalated. The officers and board of directors of Find Me and AZSTAR had injected themselves into the matter and a growing list of legal representatives was involved. Apparently from Snyder's e-mails the attorneys for Looking Up Productions were now getting involved.

One of the key reasons for writing a contract and for maintaining an up-to-date file of correspondence, e-mails and other materials is to put yourself in a position to defend yourself, your work, and your reputation when legal action is threatened.

Again, Snyder and the officers and board of directors were later offered an opportunity to make their case in a binding legal environment. Their non-response response was interesting and will be covered in a later chapter.

*Reference to *Pounding the Ground*, a documentary on the Find Me organization in which I appear.

CHAPTER ELEVEN
Enter Looking Up Productions

The July 16, 2015 e-mail and the letter from AZSTAR brings in Denise Goodwin-Pace and her firm Looking Up Productions. The firm produced a documentary called *Pounding the Ground* and was attempting to negotiate a television series based on psychic detecting. I am or perhaps now *was* in a good bit of the documentary.

"Also be advised that Denise Goodwin-Pace has notified her attorneys about this book issue with you, since you have also signed a "shopping agreement" with her (Article 4.1) that does not allow you to say or do anything without her express permission. I have been granted rights to write a book about Find Me...." (Appendix 4)

The July 29, 2015 letter from Jaburg/Wilk attorneys from Snyder and Find Me, Inc. stated in part, "Moreover, I note that you are currently subject to an agreement with Denise Goodwin Pace that restricts your ability to write about Mr. Snyder without prior written approval. Contract damages may also be available to Ms. Pace if you violate that agreement." (Appendix 23)

Concerning that "shopping agreement," Article 4.1 states in full, "Artist agrees to serve as talent on the Series for so long as Producer desires to continue to engage Artist. Artist shall be considered to serve as talent on any spin-offs or derivative projects of the Series, with terms to be negotiated in good faith but no less favorable than those set forth herein."

Apparently the board of directors and officers and/or Snyder contacted Looking Up Productions in such a manner that the firm felt a need to contact their attorneys about the book. I never heard anything from those attorneys.

The only comment I ever received from Denise Pace or Looking Up Productions regarding the book was positive. "Because Pounding the Ground is in the works about Find Me, I think it gives you some momentum for a better book deal and I'd like to see you capitalize on that in advance of our TV deal." The e-mail also stated, "These are your decisions to make, they don't affect me, but I wanted to try to assist if I can." (e-mail, Denise Goodwin-Pace to Snyder and Baldwin, February 1, 2013). (Appendix 24)

A few comments are in order.

Find Me – The Casebook was started in 2009. The agreement with Looking Up Productions was dated August 27, 2012.

The term of the agreement was 18 months.

If one co-author was in violation of such an agreement, both co-authors were in violation. From her e-mail, it is clear that Denise Goodwin-Pace and Looking Up Productions supported the project at least as of 2013.

At the time this became an issue I had been removed from the membership of Find Me and was no longer bound by any agreement anyway.

Lesson Learned: A co-author may claim exclusive rights to a story, but his or her wishes are not your command.

CHAPTER TWELVE

Enter the Cynthia Cannell Agency

A Find Me board member arranged an introduction to Cynthia Connell of the Cynthia Connell Literary Agency in New York in 2010. Snyder sent an early and very rough draft to her as a work in progress on January 21, 2010. Again, note that this e-mail is in direct conflict with Snyder's claim that he began the work after 2011 or 1012. (Appendix 18)

Find Me II – The Casebook was an on-and-off project and didn't really become a complete draft until years later. Near the end of the project we deleted a number of chapters because they were inconclusive or featured a lack of success. I wrote seven new chapters, which required input and commentary from Snyder according to our agreement – input which he never provided. This will become an important fact in a later chapter.

I sent a draft to Cannell on February 21, 2015, noting that the work was an incomplete rough draft. Snyder was copied in on the e-mail and therefore had the attached manuscript file including the 2009 Baldwin/Snyder copyright notice. This, too, is an important fact explained later. (Appendix 25)

On April 12, 2014 Snyder e-mailed "I am waiting for a response from Cynthia which should give me some direction... nothing has changed.,.. *she wants me to do the book on my own and I am doing my best to figure you into this equation!!*" (emphasis mine – grammar/spelling in the original). (Appendix 21)

The following day I responded, "We've already written Find Me

II. There's no way you can do it on your own. No matter how you look at it, she is talking about an entirely separate book. I say go for it, but this one is basically ready to go. For a number of sound reasons we need to get this book into the marketplace now."
(Appendix 26, paragraph three)

E-mail correspondence continued throughout that morning.

Snyder responded, "Hold off until I can sort this out..... "She is out of the country and returns on the 23rd.... she wants to talk then, so stand by until then..."
(Appendix 26)
(Appendix 27)

I responded, "I'll hold off until the end of the month on cleaning up the new chapters. After a lot of thinking on this, I don't see how you can sort out what appears to be unsortable. FIND ME II is done and essentially ready to go. The book she wants you to write is entirely different book and you can't morph this one into that one for lots of sound reasons. I'm not against you writing another book. In fact, I'll be glad to help any way I can if you want. Like I said, go for it. This specific little piggy just needs to get to market and soon."

As the correspondence continued notice how the Baldwin and Snyder book becomes a Snyder book. The line "She wants me to do my own book" is telling. Snyder wrote, "The chapters that I would want in the separate book are also some of the chapters that you are referring to also .. I don't know which of those chapters (cases) I would select, so that is what I am trying to sort out... It's not a different book, it is the same book only in my way of doing it with "some" of the same cases..... that is what I am trying to deal with..."

Notice also that the book is now a "separate book" and at the same time "Not a different book." (Appendix 28)

My response to that e-mail followed an hour later. "You will still need to rewrite all those chapters in your voice. That, by definition, is new material. Those chapters as currently written belong to Dan Baldwin and Kelly Snyder and are part of the Find Me II book. You can't just take them and dump them into another book. That won't work. We need to wrap this book and get it out there now. You can draft your version and roll with that." (Appendix 28)

From his e-mails it is clear that Snyder signed his own contract with the Cynthia Cannell Literary Agency and that his co-author was not part of the arrangement. (e-mail Snyder to Baldwin on May 8, 2015) "… she sent *me* a contract…" (my emphasis) My response that day was, "If the contract is for our book I need to see a copy of it. If it's for the Kelly book, no need. I'll wrap the grammar/spelling check on the new chapters this weekend."

When queried about the status of that contract on June 17, 2015, Snyder responded, "…Cynthia is rewriting the contract offer… so… waiting for the updated contract to arrive..!!..??" (grammar/spelling in the original)
(Appendix 29)
(Appendix 30)

On July 8, 2017 Snyder e-mailed in reference to the co-founder issue and *Find Me II – The Casebook*, "Thanks for handling this with understanding and professionalism .. hoping we can iron out the other issue ASAP, since I am sitting a contract with Cynthia…" (Appendix 5)

The Bottom Line: the manuscript of *Find Me II – The Casebook* by Dan Baldwin and Kelly Snyder was sent to the Cannell Agency in late February, 2015. By early April, 2015 Snyder had signed a contract with that agent for a book about Find Me cases using at least some of the same material in *Find Me II – The Casebook*

His co-author was left out of the picture.

The co-founder issue did not surface until later in the year.

Lesson Learned: an agreement with a co-author should include a description of responsibilities which includes who is responsible for marketing the project. When writing up a co-author agreement, write a precise description of the work.

Do as I say, not as I did.

CHAPTER THIRTEEN

While Snyder pursued his separate-but-not-different book, I informed him that I would pursue our original goal – publish *Find Me II – The Casebook*. I said so verbally and in writing, stating clearly that I would honor our 50/50 agreement.

> *July 9, 2015*
>
> *Kelly,*
>
> *Your recent telephone conversations and e-mails have astounded me. I am heartsick that you have so misconstrued at this late date the development of our book project, Find Me II – The Casebook. I would have responded to your last two e-mails more quickly, but I really was shaken by your words and I also wanted to double check my records to verify some of the facts stated below. Clearly, your memory and your facts as stated are seriously flawed. To set the record straight here is what is and what was.*
>
> *What Is.*
>
> *When you abandoned our project earlier this year (for example, not responding to repeated requests for your input) to pursue a contract for your own book with the agent Cynthia Cannell, you left me with the responsibility of finishing the project and that is what I have done.*
>
> *Find Me II – The Casebook is now in e-mail and paperback formats and will be available no later than early next week (possibly by this weekend) through Amazon (Kindle), Smashwords, Barnes & Noble, CreateSpace and other distributors. As I said, I write to publish, not to sit on a project and not to give it away.*

I e-mailed last month that I was moving on to complete the project. You used the term "takeover" in your most recent e-mail. That is an inaccurate and unfortunate term. I have simply finished a project we started – just as I said I would do. Again, (1) your abandonment of the project, (2) your seeking of your own project on the same subject, and (3) the overlong length of time involved in this project were contributing factors to wrapping this up at this time.

What was.

Your statement that our project began in 2011 or 2012 with me agreeing to help write your book in your voice is in error.

I approached you in 2009 about co-writing a book on Find Me cases and you accepted.

This was always a co-author project. There was no mention of this being "your" book or a "Kelly Snyder" book.

The project isn't and has never been a Find Me organization project. It's a Dan Baldwin and Kelly Snyder project.

As you know, every title page from day one has been slugged "Dan Baldwin and Kelly Snyder."

There was no discussion and certainly no decision to write the casebook in your voice. This was never a ghostwriting project.

In 2009 we discussed the writing style to be used and agreed that I would write in the standard style used on most of my ghostwriting projects for business books and that was used in the as-told-to book I wrote on Find Me with some of our original group.

In your e-mail (7/6/15) you mentioned a meeting where we discussed writing a book in your voice and that I offered to help you with it. I have absolutely no recollection of such a meeting or any such discussion. Even assuming faulty memory on my part, a book in your voice discussed at that time was clearly a separate book (a term you used in an e-mail to me on the subject) and not Find Me II – The Casebook.

(I offered to help you write a book in your voice, but that offer was made this year and in direct reference to the book you're working on with Cynthia. That offer stands.)

The first time the theme of writing in your voice came up was in mid-April this year when you e-mailed me that Cynthia wanted you to do your own book in your own voice.

That's the timeframe in which you abandoned our project and started seeking your own. I offered my support for your new project, but noted that you could not take our project and put your name on it or modify it for that purpose. The information in Find Me II is not proprietary, but the form in which it is presented is. You are free to write your own version in your own words.

I use the term abandon accurately. I have for months requested your input on the newest chapters – those suggested by Joni. You have never responded despite my repeated requests.

I asked if you wanted to update your photo or bio for the back cover, but, again, you did not respond.

I mentioned an estimate for the hard costs of producing the book and splitting them. Again, there was no response. (Those costs are minimal and within the range I mentioned to you.)

When I mentioned the deal I negotiated for the front cover photo and front cover design (we got both for gratis from a national award winning graphic designer), you made no comment, not even a request to see the design.

Last month I e-mailed you that I was pushing ahead

with completion of the project and that is what I have done. Of course, our 50/50 profit split agreement stands.

I am surprised and saddened by your recent abandonment of a book we have worked on for so long, but I do wish you the best of luck with your other book.

The bottom line in all of this is that Find Me II – The Casebook is, after six years of labor, finally in the marketplace. I have faith that it will do well.

Dan

(Emphasis added) *(Appendix 32)*

The notice of my removal, which came from Snyder on July 14, 2015, included:

"This notice is also to advise you that I do not want any part or portion of the book that you have decided you are co-author. Do not publish anything that suggests or infers that I have written or stated anything that promotes the book. My name cannot be on the cover supporting this book."

Snyder, speaking for the officers and board of directors of the Find Me organization, wrote an e-mail to me on July 16, 2015. Included in that e-mail:

"Your stance on the fact that you believe you can publish a book about Find Me is another board issue, but has to do with our legal stance on how we will address your actions. If you proceed with the book without my consent then it is something the courts will ultimately decide… You can call the book anything you want, just don't call it Find Me or mention it is about Find Me investigations or that I am agreeing to anything about it being published."

(Appendix 4)

On July 17 in response to my message of July 14, 2015 stating that I took him at his word in not wanting any part of the book, Snyder wrote, "It's yours to keep, just make sure there are NO references that I have anything to do with it and that NONE of my comments are in the book. Find Me name cannot be made reference to either or that this is sanctioned by Find Me. My attorney will be sending you a confirmation of all of this, so there are NO misunderstandings…" (grammar/spelling in the original) (Appendix 33)

The message was clear. Snyder demanded to be completely disassociated with *Find Me II – The Casebook.*

That should have ended an unfortunate and unnecessary wrap up to *Find Me II – The Casebook.*

The letter from the Find Me attorney that arrived indicated that it was not.

CHAPTER FOURTEEN

A letter from the legal firm of Jaburg/Wilk dated July 29, 2015 arrived in my snail-mail box. The firm represented Find Me, Inc. and Kelly Snyder. Again, note that the officers and board of directors had injected themselves into an issue between Snyder and Baldwin. Snyder *and* the officers and board of directors were claiming copyright to the work. The letter made a number of accusations, which were unsupported and unsupportable. It also contained a number of censorship demands.

The letter is printed in its entirety in the Appendix 34. It was slugged:

Re: Copyright Infringement – Find Me

The letter made a number of statements.

"This firm represents Kelly Snyder and Find Me, Inc. in connection with the protection and enforcement of their intellectual property rights...."

"You have since claimed that you 'copyrighted' the book, including Mr. Snyder's portion and that you intended to move forward with publishing the book on your own...

"Mr. Snyder retains the copyrights in the material he created/authored... Mr. Snyder independently authored 17 of the chapters in the draft of the book...

"Mr. Snyder also created various audio recordings in connection with the book for which he similarly retains copyrights..."

Removing all the legalese, the letter from the Find Me attorney states:

I copyrighted or threatened to copyright the book under my own name.

This is an untruth.

Snyder provided copyrighted audio recordings for use in the book.

This is an untruth.

Snyder independently wrote 17 chapters of the book.

This is an untruth.

Each of these claims is addressed in following chapters.

For now, note that in response to this letter the officers and board of directors, through their attorney, were offered the opportunity to document those claims in a legally-binding arbitration by an independent judge. They could place their documentation on the table and I would place mine on the same table. The judge would evaluate the material and make a final decision. (Appendix 35)

Although repeated, the offer was never answered.

I responded through their attorney that their lack of response indicated a lack of faith in their claims. I would proceed with publication while honoring Snyder's demand to be disassociated with the project. There was no response to this letter either. (Appendix 36)
(Appendix 42)

I proceeded with production.

Now, as to those claims….

CHAPTER FIFTEEN

I Would Copyright the Book on My Own – Wrong.

The claim is ludicrous for one simple reason: *Find Me II – The Casebook* was already copyrighted by Dan Baldwin and Kelly Snyder and had been so since 2009. The authors were fully protected by the copyright laws of the United States.

Why the officers and board of directors of Find Me would make such a claim while in possession of documents showing just the opposite is beyond me.

Let me be clear about this. I never said, wrote, e-mailed, or even hinted that I would copyright *Find Me II – The Casebook* under my own name. That statement is false. Before making such a statement, the officers and board of directors should have considered a number of obvious factors.

The first page typed in 2009 was the title sheet, which included notice that the work was copyrighted by Dan Baldwin and Kelly Snyder. The copyright remained in force until Snyder demanded to be removed as an author/co-author from the project. (Appendix 33)

Remember from the previous chapter that I was proceeding with publication (honoring the 50/50 agreement) and had prepared *Find Me II – The Casebook* for publication as an e-book and paperback.

The title page from that work read as follows.

FIND ME II

THE CASEBOOK

Authentic Stories of Psychic Detecting

Dan Baldwin & Kelly Snyder

The About the Authors page lists Dan Baldwin (as an inaugural member) and Kelly Snyder and this notice appears at the bottom of the page.

A Four Knights Press Publication

Copyright © 2015 by Dan Baldwin and Jerry "Kelly" Snyder

(Appendix 37)

Snyder knew (and the board should have known) that he had not been removed as a co-author. He received two e-mail updates on June 23, 2015 on that subject.

"I'm working on a new cover now. The old cover w/new title is the back up."

"Also, if you want a new photo or updated author cover comment, I need a jpeg and copy ASAP."

The old cover reference is to the second printing of the first FIND ME book which had Baldwin and Snyder bios on the back cover. (That's the back cover stating I am a "founder" of Find Me, which had been in print since 2011.)

There never was a reason, any reason, for Snyder or the officers and board of directors to think that I would attempt to copyright the work under my own name.

The officers and board of directors should have been well aware of this at least no later than June 27, 2015 when I e-mailed Snyder a progress report on the cover.

> "…The back cover and spine from the first book will serve for this one… I'll send the manuscript in for formatting (e-book and paperback) in one week. If you can, get me you (sic) comments on the new chapters." The back cover of the as-told-to book list Baldwin and Snyder under an "About the Authors" subtitle.
> (Appendix 38)
> (Appendix 12)

Just to ram home the point, I had the book formatted for ebook and paperback, a cover designed, and had uploaded the work to distributors. It was ready for immediate publication. The front cover read:

FIND ME II
The Casebook
By
Dan Baldwin
And
Kelly Snyder

The spine of the paperback version read:
FIND ME II The Casebook Dan Baldwin & Kelly Snyder

The back cover contained the bios of Dan Baldwin and Kelly Snyder. (Appendix 39)

As noted earlier, the book was ready for immediate distribution through the usual online outlets. A sample of the Kindle promotional page can be seen in the Appendix. The paperback version was also ready for immediate distribution through CreateSpace. (Appendix 41& 41b)

Does this look like an author copyrighting a product under his own name to you?

Why the officers and board of directors would make such a claim when in possession of or certainly access to documentation of their error is a mystery to me.

The Bottom Line: The statement from the officers and board of directors of Find Me that I said I was going to copyright *Find Me II – The Casebook* under my own name is false.

CHAPTER SIXTEEN

Snyder Provided Copyrighted Audio Recordings – Wrong.

In the letter from their attorney the officers and board of directors of Find Me state, "Mr. Snyder also created various audio recordings in connection with the book, for which he similarly retains copyrights."

Snyder did not create any audio recordings. He did not provide me with any copyrighted audio recordings. Neither he nor the board nor their attorney produced a copyright notice, recordings, transcripts or other documentation to back up the erroneous claim.

The claim probably refers to the two interviews I conducted with Snyder to record his memories and impressions on certain chapters. I recorded these sessions on my personal hand-held digital recorder. The recordings were never copyrighted because they consisted of raw data which was to be used in a book already under copyright. If there is a copyright issue it would be one of dual copyright to the material. Snyder is free to use the raw data as he sees fit, but not the presentation of that material as in *How Find Me Lost Me.*

Again, one wonders why the officers and board of directors would state a claim of copyright where none exists.

CHAPTER SEVENTEEN

Snyder Independently Wrote 17 Chapters of Find Me II – The Casebook – Wrong.

The letter from the Find Me attorney also states, "Mr. Snyder independently authored 17 of the chapters in the draft of the book."

Mr. Snyder did not.

He wrote a draft of one chapter, which I rewrote for publication. That chapter was pulled from the final version of the book as he demanded. He did not independently write 17 chapters. He did not even honor his commitment to provide comment on seven of the chapters in the final version.

The officers and board of directors were offered the opportunity to back up the claim in a legally binding environment.

"Mr. Baldwin prefers the appointment of an independent third party to act as editor/judge/arbitrator to determine authorship. To aid in that evaluation, the arbitrator should receive manuscripts and other material to assist him/her in determining whether the book is written as 'two voice' or a single voice. Each party would also be required to authenticate those chapters that they have claimed to have written.

I suggested to Mr. Baldwin that he and Mr. Snyder could present work samples from some of the published works that each has authored or co-authored, for comparison of the manuscript for this recent work." (Appendix 42)

This should have been easy for the officers and board. They had made a number of claims, claims which they were given the opportunity to prove in a legally binding environment. Such an action would have settled the matter once and for all. The officers and board of directors never responded to this offer.

There is another matter to consider regarding their claim that Snyder independently wrote 17 chapters of the book. That feat is physically impossible.

One of the group's members read and the manuscript and recommended eliminating several chapters that were inconclusive or unsuccessful and replacing them with cases with positive outcomes. I wrote seven new chapters. Snyder's responsibility was to provide his input into these chapters. He abandoned the project after signing an agreement with the Cannell Agency and did not respond to my repeated requests for that input.

"We recently gutted the original to replace about half the chapters which were interesting but with undetermined or unsuccessful outcomes... These seven chapters require Kelly's insight and commentary and the above mentioned work on my end." (Appendix 2)

"In other news, I'd like to wrap the book up in April. I can driver (sic) to your place for an interview on the remaining chapters... or we could do that by phone..." (Appendix 21 – read through multiple e-mails)

"I'll start the rewrite on the new chapters today and will wrap by the end of the week. All we'll need then is your comments on the new chapters." (Appendix 27)

"I'll be working on our book this week and will finish the grammar/spelling/style review of the new chapters. All we will need is your input on those chapters." (Appendix 26)

"I still need your comments on the new chapters, but you will have to make time to get those to me. If you want we can do that by telephone interview. It shouldn't take a long time." (Appendix 14)

"Regarding your comments on the new chapters in Find Me II: I can't put in what you won't provide. Please get those to me or the book will have to be published as is. It will be better with your comments." (Appendix 43)

"I use the term abandon accurately. I have for months requested your input on the newest chapters – those suggested by Joni. You have never responded despite my repeated requests." (Appendix 32)

"I'll send the manuscript in for formatting (e-book and paperback) in one week. If you can, get me you (sic) comments on the new chapters." (Appendix 44)

That input was never provided.

The bottom line: Regarding copyright and authorship, the officers and board of directors of Find Me were grossly in error. Snyder did not independently write 17 chapters of the book.

CHAPTER EIGHTEEN

I informed Snyder by e-mail directly and the officers and board of directors through their attorney that their lack of response indicated that all their concerns had been addressed and that I was moving ahead with publication of a renamed *Find Me II – The Casebook*. Again, there was no response from the officers and board of directors, Snyder or the attorney for Find Me.

Again, it must be noted that I offered to settle the copyright issue, the audio recordings issue, and the authorship issue in a legally binding arbitration. That the officers and board of directors of Find Me chose not to respond to the opportunity to back up their claims should be considered significant.

(Appendix 45)

(Appendix 46)

Chapter Nineteen

Lessons Learned

"A verbal contract isn't worth the paper it's written on."

Whether or not Sam Goldwyn actually said that, the expression is true.

As I wrote in the beginning of this book, the one project I just knew I would not need a contract for was the *Find Me II – The Casebook* project. The breach of trust that followed proves the folly of ignoring Goldwyn's advice.

Write a well-thought out contract on any co-author project before you begin any serious work. Do not automatically assume that you are working with an honorable person or persons. Things change. And they may change for reasons you never know. I do not mean for you to be automatically suspicious of your partners, only that you should remember the words of President Ronald Reagan. "Trust, but verify."

Have a lawyer review the contract. The law can be complex and confusing. Attorneys and the courts have their own language. We call it "legalese." You'll need someone experienced with the territory to help you avoid the legal landmines.

Document your work. Keep accurate files in multiple locations of all your work. Make paper copies and keep them organized.

Record your correspondence. Keep multiple copies of your agreements, letters, e-mails and notes scribbled on cocktail napkins. If and when a "he said/she said" situation arises you should be in a position to say, "Okay, regardless of what you say now, this is what you wrote then."

CHAPTER TWENTY
Choices for the Co-Author

When confronted with a situation such as the one outlined in this book, the co-author has a number of options.

One: like it and lump it. He can kiss goodbye all his time, energy, money, effort and heart and move on to something else.

Two: try to work out the situation. In this case the working it out process involved direct communication with the parties involved, a mediation service and eventually a legal firm. None of those efforts worked.

Three: publish the work according to your agreement. Definitely consult an attorney before proceeding with this step. As an author you have rights. In the case outlined here my attempts to publish under the original agreement were thwarted by other parties. The attempt to prevent publication, however, was not. And that's how *Find Me II – The Casebook by Dan Baldwin and Kelly Snyder* became *They Are Not Yet Lost by Dan Baldwin*.

Four: Go public. We live in an age of social media and of virtually instant publication. Provided you have documentation and that you stick to the facts, state your case on social media. In this situation I sent documented e-mail messages to select people within the organization offering to provide copies of the documentation as I had originally offered the same to the Find Me board. At least the information was received by some people in the organization.

Five: Print. The hard costs of publishing an e-book and paperback combo are amazingly inexpensive; the process of publication is easy and remarkably fast. There has never been a better time for writers seeking publication than right now. For example, once this manuscript is completed it will be available in e-book and paperback in more than 80 countries around the world – and in a remarkably short amount of time.

If your story justifies the effort, your story can be told.

Do as I say.

Do as I did.

Tell it.

APPENDIX

The documentation in the Appendix isn't presented in chronological order. Often a single e-mail will refer to more than one topic. Refer to the Appendix number as you read the book to follow the events.

Appendix 1

The removal notice. All three paragraphs are important in chapters that follow. Note here Snyder's demand to be removed as an author/co-author, the pending involvement of the Find Me lawyer, and the threat to notify Amazon.

Dan Baldwin

From:	"kelly snyder" <kilomonster1@gmail.com>
To:	"Dan" <baldco@msn.com>
Sent:	Tuesday, July 14, 2015 7:55 AM
Subject:	Find Me

Dan,

You have been removed from Find Me as a Board member and regular member. The board decided that you violated all five of the Code of Ethics by your statement that you are a co-founder of Find Me. Truthfulness is the key component of this action, not my sensitivities.

This notice is also to advise you that I do not want any part or portion of the book,that you have decided you are co-author. Do not publish anything that suggests or infers that I have written or stated anything that promotes this book. My name cannot be on the cover supporting this book.

My new attorney Maria Crimi Speth will be sending you a confirmation of this request and details surrounding this request. Any reference that you are a co-founder of Find Me on Amazon also needs to be removed. My attorney will also be including Amazon in our correspondence.

J.E. "Kelly" Snyder
CEO/FOUNDER - FIND ME

Appendix 2

Notice of Baldwin's removal to the membership. There is no notice that the removal was held at a separate and special call meeting of the board – a meeting that violated the 501c3 (IRS) bylaws of the non-profit corporation.

FM- BOARD MEETING 09/27/2015

Ideas are needed regarding fundraising events, so please provide those to Peggy & Michelle once you make contact with them. Ask five or your friends to provide and identify for you corporations or businesses or both that are looking to support a non-profit organization like ours. Their contribution will help find missing people, solve homicides and identify human trafficking networks for their tax write-off. You are not asking your friends for money, but instead for ideas. Please pass to Kelly and he will provide this information to the R&D Team.

Artificial intelligence System - See Above

Japan TV docu series will continue with another investigation and search in November. Our TV airing in June on the YUUKI ONOSHI investigation ranked our program as number #2 in prime time ratings. We assume that is why they asked us back for another episode..!!

Might be going back to Georgia to search again for Chase Massner with new information revealed that is a high probability. Waiting for law enforcement response.

Member Dan Baldwin was removed from the FM Group and Board of Directors for violating the code of ethics.

He was replaced by Scott Snyder as board President.

AZ-STaR continues to be extremely supportive of our efforts in search and rescue. We are entering our 14th year as partners.

Still seeking a volunteer to take the Treasurer position on the Board of Directors. Please contact Kelly if interested.

Looking for Private Investigator(s) to join our team, please contact Kelly with your suggestions.

Stacey and Nathan Fields continue testing the new psychic applicants. Testing system is working well. Have turned down 20 psychics through the system and approved 12 new members.

Michelle Durnell is researching a custom made Find Me Bracelet to be given as a keepsake for donors, families of victims. Once we have a prototype it will be displayed for your viewing pleasure.

The Legacy Foundation located in Arizona will be partnering with Find Me to put on a Golf Tournament with local golf pros at a fundraising event in 2016. We will keep you updated on its progress. Victims' families will be invited and presented with a lifetime Legacy Award and their loved one honored and memorialized forever.

Sunny Dawn Johnston - Secretary

Appendix 3

Find Me is a non-profit corporation operating within the meaning of Section 501c3 of the Internal Revenue Code of 1986. The bylaws specifically require that a board member to be notified of and be allowed to be heard at a board meeting for removal. No such notification was made. No opportunity to be heard was allowed. As noted in the chapters, this violation represents a pattern of action by the officers and board of directors and is not a single incident.

Find Me, Inc   EIN 45-3647310

(a) All directors shall be elected to serve a one-year term, however the term may be extended until a successor has been elected.

(b) Director terms shall be staggered so that approximately half the number of directors will end their terms in any given year.

(c) Directors may serve terms in succession.

(d) The term of office shall be considered to begin January 1 and end December 31 of the second year in office, unless the term is extended until such time as a successor has been elected.

4.04 Qualifications and Election of Directors

In order to be eligible to serve as a director on the board of directors, the individual must be 18 years of age and an affiliate within affiliate classifications created by the board of directors. Directors may be elected at any board meeting by the majority vote of the existing board of directors. The election of directors to replace those who have fulfilled their term of office shall take place in January of each year.

4.05 Vacancies

The board of directors may fill vacancies due to the expiration of a director's term of office, resignation, death, or removal of a director or may appoint new directors to fill a previously unfilled board position, subject to the maximum number of directors under these Bylaws.

(a) Unexpected Vacancies. Vacancies in the board of directors due to resignation, death, or removal shall be filled by the board for the balance of the term of the director being replaced.

4.06 Removal of Directors

A director other than the Founder/CEO or Other Founding Directors may be removed by two-thirds (⅔) vote of the board of directors then in office, if:

(a) the director is absent and unexcused from two or more meetings of the board of directors in a twelve month period. The board president is empowered to excuse directors from attendance for a reason deemed adequate by the board president. The president shall not have the power to excuse him/herself from the board meeting attendance and in that case, the board vice president shall excuse the president. Or:

(b) for cause or no cause, if before any meeting of the board at which a vote on removal will be made the director in question is given electronic or written notification of the board's intention to discuss her/his case and is given the opportunity to be heard at a meeting of the board.

Other Founding Directors may be removed by a two-thirds (⅔) vote of the board of directors then in office and the Founder.

The Founder/CEO of Find Me, Inc. may only be removed by a court of law with jurisdiction in the state of Arizona. A court of law may only remove the Founder if found to be mentally, emo-

---

Appendix 4

Find Me – The Casebook is an issue.

I never received verbally or in writing "cease and desist order" from Snyder mentioned on page two.

Notice Snyder's peculiar interpretation of the 501c3 (IRS) bylaws, also on page two.

Dan Baldwin

From:	"kelly snyder" <kilomonster1@gmail.com>
To:	"Dan Baldwin" <baldco@centurylink.net>
Cc:	<kilomonster@centurylink.net>; <sunndawn@cox.net>; "Dave Campbell" <theastrologystore@gmail.com>; "John DenBoer" <jwdenboer@yahoo.com>; "Scott" <quailhunter@seanet.com>; "Peggy Rometo" <peg.rometo@gmail.com>; "Dan Baldwin" <baldco@msn.com>
Sent:	Thursday, July 16, 2015 2.02 PM
Subject:	Re: A Request to the Board of Directors of Find Me

DAN-BOARD

The Find Me Book is also at issue here, but may lead into legal action, so it was left out of the equation for determining you being removed.

You mentioned you thought I was being to sensitive about the co-founder issue, this action for your removal was taken because of your lack of truthfulness and the integrity of our group is at stake.

I have personally "never" heard you use that term co-founder in my presence. It was only recently brought to my attention while at the NYC fundraiser. It was not something that I acted upon then, because I didn't hear you say it. My mistake, was not addressing it at that time. Using that term begs the question if whether or not it is truthful, not something that you were able to get away with for a long period of time. By your definition; if no one hears it or questions it then it must be true and what is the harm…? The fact that you corrected it does not negate the fact that you were being untruthful. You should not be proud of that fact or use as an argument that you have been untruthful for a decade. If you had asked me, the answer would have been NO, since you had absolutely nothing to do with the idea/concept or creation of Find Me. For the record: Find Me was created three months before I met you. If any of the Find Me members or Board members have heard you make the statement you are a co-founder, I would be shocked and amazed, since In 12 years I have never heard you say it. If any member has heard you make that statement, then they should come forward in your defense and I welcome their input.

Your stance on the fact that you believe you can publish a book about Find Me is another board issue, but has to do with our legal stance on how we will address your actions. If you proceed with the book without my consent then it is something the courts will ultimately decide. The Find Me Trademark is owned by me and you have been advised of this fact. You have also been advised that my name cannot be used to represent that I have written anything in the book if you publish it. You can call the book anything you want, just don't call it Find Me or mention it is about Find Me investigations or that I am agreeing to anything about it being published.

Also be advised that Denise Goodwin-Pace has notified her attorneys about this book issue with you, since you have also signed a "shopping agreement" with her (Article 4.1) that does not allow you to say or do anything without her express permission. I have been granted rights to write a book about Find Me, but you have not. You are not a co-author as you are suggesting. You asked if you could assist me, but that verbal agreement was not authorizing you being a co-author. Is it just me or does there seem to be a pattern developing here…?

Continued on next page

Bottom Line is that you were removed for one violation which broke all five of our Code of Ethics. My appreciation and response to you for handling that matter professionally was sincere, but does not negate the violation, nor wipe out our obligation as board members to address the violation. It is your continued attitude and terminology that "you will be going forward with the book" even tho I have asked that you cease and desist verbally and in an email to you. It is that type of attitude that makes me believe your are not being forthright and suggests a pattern being developed here.

Since you were a volunteer and we are a non-profit there are no requirements to advise you prior to the board making their decision for termination. The facts have been provided and the board can way all of the facts and decide without your input. They also can ask you if you did in fact violate our Code of Ethics and make their decision on your answer. You admitted your guilt to this violation. You have a right to state your feelings, but have no grounds to contest a board decision. Several members have been removed while you were a board member and these are the same guidelines we used for your termination.

The board can consider if your termination is temporary or permanent and they decided to remove your permanently. If they decide to 'reconsider' based on your email today then that is solely up to them. I just presented the facts to them and they voted. I do not have a vote in these matters, unless there is a tie or other extenuating circumstances. The board can respond to you directly, but must include their response to other board members and I encourage that, if they decide to revisit this issue.

Final Note: You make light of the fact that in various areas of books, websites, meetings you have lied about being co-founder as a "convenience describing your length of service" and insinuate that it must be OK if no one objects or challenges you on this issue. A lie is still a lie regardless of your intent. What you are not considering or mentioning is that I trusted you for 12 years to not only abide by our Rules, Guidelines and Code of Ethics, but with this long-term trust, came friendship and never did it enter my mind that I had or would want to monitor your statements or mistrust you in any capacity. I would never have expected anything like this from you, therefore I trusted you implicitly. Now this trust is broken and I personally can 'never' trust you again. To take advantage of someone's trust and friendship is something I won't and do not have to tolerate.

J.E. "Kelly" Snyder
CEO/FOUNDER

On Jul 16, 2015, at 8:44 AM, Dan Baldwin <baldco@centurylink.net> wrote:

Dan Baldwin   July 16, 2015

A statement for the board of directors of Find Me.

I was informed on July 14, 2015 that I was removed from the board of directors and the Find Me organization for using the term "co-founder" of Find Me. This action was taken without my knowledge – I was an active board member at that time – and I was not allowed to provide input into the decision making process. In the interest of fairness and basic courtesy, I ask that the following be entered into the minutes at the next Find Me board of directors meeting

Appendix 5

Again, the book is mentioned as an issue.

Dan Baldwin

From:	"kelly snyder" <kilomonster1@gmail.com>
To:	"Dan Baldwin" <baldco@msn.com>
Sent:	Wednesday, July 8, 2015 8:10 AM
Subject:	Re: Co-Founder reverence

For the record.... I have only heard you make that reference in recent months ... it bothered me then, but really only mattered when you started putting it in print... I also didn't notice you had it in your bio which I am having removed.... I have trusted you for so long things like this did not ever need my attention.!!

I am not all that sensitive, but this issue and the book issue made it seem almost like a hostile take-over and that would affect me with Denise and other "business" and personal related items in play...

Thanks for handling this with understanding and professionalism .. hoping we can iron out the other issue ASAP, since I am sitting on a contract with Cynthia ' .. Thursday will work....

Kelly

On Jul 7, 2015, at 4:06 PM, Dan Baldwin <baldco@msn.com> wrote:

Dan Baldwin
Author Co-Author Ghostwriter
480-807-9682
www.fourknightspress.com www.danbaldwin.biz

Kelly,

I have pulled the co-founder reference off the Practical Pendulum
e-book. Any further paperback orders will also show inaugural member.

I've used that term for more than a decade and in your presence. If
it bothered you, all you had to do was ask. No biggie.

As to your concerns about Find Me II - The Casebook, they deserve
more than a cursory response. A separate e-mail will address those
tomorrow, no later than Thursday.

Dan

Appendix 6

Another notice that the book is an issue. "They knew nothing about the book issue...." If it was an issue, why wasn't the board notified? The reference to board minutes is covered in a later chapter.

Dan Baldwin

From:	"Dan Baldwin" <baldco@centurylink.net>
To:	"kelly snyder" <kilomonster1@gmail.com>; <sunnydawn@cox.net>; <theastrologystore@gmail.com>; <jwdenboer@yahoo.com>; <quailhunter@seanet.com>; <peg.rometo@gmail.com>; <baldco@msn.com>
Sent:	Friday, July 17, 2015 1:02 PM
Subject:	Re: Find Me II - The Casebook

Kelly,

The e-mail sent to me and the board yesterday led off with, "The Find Me Book is also at issue here...."

My request that my responses to these e-mails being read into the minutes stands.

Dan

From: "kelly snyder" <kilomonster1@gmail.com>
To: "Dan Baldwin" <baldco@centurylink.net>
Sent: Friday, July 17, 2015 11:41:34 AM
Subject: Re: Find Me II - The Casebook

They knew nothing about the book issue and made their decision based on your untruthfulness.. this divagation won't work Dan, since this chapter hasn't been written yet... we are waiting for your next move. ..!

Since you are providing this to the entire board it is NOT something that needs read in to the minutes and there is no precedence for it. You are a "VOLUNTEER" .... not a paid employee...!!

On Jul 17, 2015, at 10:55 AM, Dan Baldwin <baldco@centurylink.net> wrote:

7/17/2015

Appendix 7

Notice that Snyder references my biography on the official Find Me web site in which the term co-founder is used, indicating that he (not the board) is having it moved prior to the vote from the board of directors.

Again the book is raised as an issue.

Note paragraph four on the first page and the reference to Snyder's claim that he began thinking of the book in 2011 and that it would be written 100% in his style of writing. This is a grossly inaccurate statement be addressed in a later chapter of this book.

Page 1 of 1

Dan Baldwin

From:	"kelly snyder" <kilomonster1@gmail.com>
To:	"Dan" <baldco@msn.com>
Sent:	Monday, July 6, 2015 8.34 AM
Subject:	Find Me Group

Dan,

Friendship aside, I need to discuss two things that have been bothering me for quite some time. You have been telling people and recently put into print on your book stating you are a co-founder of Find Me. You are not a co-founder. You are a inaugural member and board member. That would be an accurate and appropriate statement and one I am happy to support.

You must remove this statement from your book immediately.

There also needs to be clarity about my book and its content. I want to remind you how the start of book two unfolded.

I decided in 2011 to write another book, but 100% in my style of writing. Later that year or in early 2012 you asked if I was considering writing another book. I stated at that time I was considering it, but again repeated that it was going to be in my style. You stated " if you need or want my help I would be glad to help you."

With that said, I stated I would someday figure out the direction of the book. Co-authorship was never mentioned. You agreed to help me, but now I am getting the distinct impression you see yourself as co-author. I cannot have a co-author since my contract with Denise would not allow it. I allowed you to assist me and planned on sharing in the proceeds with you, but that is as far as it would go with your involvement. I am happy to pay you an appropriate fee for the work you have done on the book as soon as the book is sold you will receive compensation and I am happy to put this in writing.

You stated in our last conversation that you went ahead and did a copy-write procedure on the book. I am troubled by this statement as I didn't ask you to do this. It is an unnecessary step as my agent and publisher will handle this. More importantly, did you make Find Me or myself as owner? If you did not, then this needs to be corrected immediately.

I need you to honor this arrangement by taking the necessary steps to correct the above mentioned items. I will move forward with you in a clear and cohesive manner and we can also discuss this, but the last time we spoke you were less than cooperative.

I appreciate all that you have done for myself and Find Me and would like to continue our friendship and your valued role as a trusted Find Me member.

Kelly

Continued on next page

Dan Baldwin

From:	"kelly snyder" <kilomonster1@gmail.com>
To:	"Dan Baldwin" <baldco@msn.com>
Sent:	Wednesday, July 8, 2015 8:10 AM
Subject:	Re: Co-Founder reverence

For the record.... I have only heard you make that reference in recent months ... it bothered me then, but really only mattered when you started putting it in print... I also didn't notice you had it in your bio which I am having removed.... I have trusted you for so long things like this did not ever need my attention.!!

I am not all that sensitive, but this issue and the book issue made it seem almost like a hostile take-over and that would affect me with Denise and other "business" and personal related items in play...

Thanks for handling this with understanding and professionalism .. hoping we can iron out the other issue ASAP, since I am sitting on a contract with Cynthia   .. Thursday will work....

Kelly

On Jul 7, 2015, at 4:06 PM, Dan Baldwin <baldco@msn.com> wrote:

Dan Baldwin
Author Co-Author Ghostwriter
480-807-9682
www.fourknightspress.com www.danbaldwin.biz

Kelly,

I have pulled the co-founder reference off the Practical Pendulum
e-book. Any further paperback orders will also show inaugural member.

I've used that term for more than a decade and in your presence. If
it bothered you, all you had to do was ask. No biggie.

As to your concerns about Find Me II - The Casebook, they deserve
more than a cursory response. A separate e-mail will address those
tomorrow, no later than Thursday.

Dan

Appendix 8

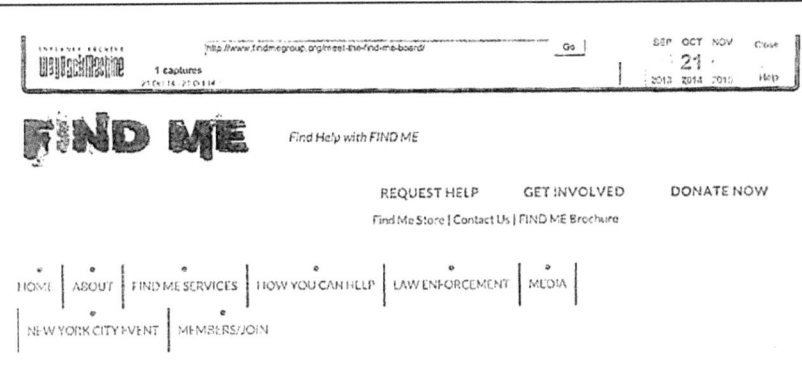

MEET THE FIND ME BOARD OF DIRECTORS

Founder/CEO
J.E. "Kelly" Snyder Jerry "Kelly" Snyder is a retired Federal Agent with 25 plus years in law enforcement. After retirement Kelly wanted to devote his time to helping children. Shortly thereafter, Kelly joined the National Center for Missing and Exploited Children (NCMEC) and also became a Big Brother with the Big Brothers Big Sisters program in Arizona. While attending the NCMEC academy Kelly met Mrs. Wetterling and Mrs. Nick who had both lost their children. This became a defining moment for Kelly because he realized he wanted to help find missing children. Kelly founded the Find Me group in 2002. The group was created to find missing children, but has evolved to finding all missing persons and resolving homicides. Supporting law enforcement and providing closure for families and individuals effected by the loss of a family member or friend is Kelly's goal.

President – Dan Baldwin Dan Baldwin, whose skill is pendulum dowsing, is a founding member of Find Me and he has participated as a "ground pounder" on numerous search and rescue missions. He is the writer of the "as told to" book *Find Me*. Dan is also the author of three Western novels, *Caldera*, *Caldera-A Man on Fire*, and *Trapp Canyon*; two mysteries, *Desecration* and *Heresy*; and a crime thriller, *Sparky and the King*. His the co-author of *Just the FAQs – About Alcohol and Drug Abuse* and is the ghostwriter of more than 50 books on business. He also writes articles and interviews for legal magazines throughout the U.S. Dan teaches a course on pendulum dowsing titled *The Practical Pendulum – A Swinger's Guide*. He has won numerous local, regional and national awards for copywriting and for directing film/video projects. He is certified in Wilderness First Aid, "plays at" the Native American flute, hikes the Superstition Mountains, and camps wherever his 4WD will take him – and get him back out. Dan says, "Being a member of Find Me is challenging, sometimes grueling, frustrating, even heartbreaking and probably the most rewarding thing I've ever done in my life."

Vice President – Dave Campbell Dave Campbell is a Certified Research Medium (WCRM) with the Windbridge Institute in Tucson, AZ. He was also a research medium with the VERITAS program from the University of Arizona with Dr. Gary Schwartz. Dave is also a professional Astrologer certified through the American Federation of Astrologers (PMAFA). Dave specializes in Forensic Astrology and wrote a book called; *Forensic Astrology Solving Crimes with Astrology*. He also owns a metaphysical bookstore in Glendale, AZ called The Astrology Store. Dave has been a psychic-medium, and forensic astrologer for Find Me since 2002. He also is a Certified Clinical Hypnotherapist (C.Ht.) Dave has been featured frequently on television regarding; astrology, psychic-medium work and locating the missing.

Appendix 9

GARY A. WOLF

LICENSED IN
ARIZONA AND COLORADO

LAW OFFICES OF

GARY A. WOLF, P.C.

459 NORTH GRANADA AVENUE
TUCSON, ARIZONA 85701
PHONE 520/622-5686
FAX 520/882-9861
E-MAIL wolf333@mindspring.com
www.attorneygarywolf.com

July 5, 2016

Ms. Maria Crimi Speth, Esq.
JABURG/WILK
3200 N. Central Avenue, 20th Floor
Phoenix, AZ 85012

RE: Dan Baldwin v. Snyder, FIND ME, et al.

Dear Ms. Crimi Speth:

Please be advised that this law firm represents Dan Baldwin in his claims against your clients for defamation, false light invasion of privacy and violation of the Arizona Corporation Code and IRC Section 501(c)(3). This correspondence is subject to Arizona Rule of Evidence 408 and corresponding federal rule.

In your July 29, 2015 letter, you claimed Mr. Baldwin "copyrighted" a co-authored book *"on his own,"* insinuating that he engaged in copyright infringement by not including your client's name as the co-author of a co-created, co-researched and co-written work. In fact, Mr. Baldwin always included your client as a co-author, since both Mr. Baldwin and your client co-created the work. You also misquoted the law as it applies to co-authored works, whereas either author can register and publish the work, so long as both authors are named and both receive their pro rata compensation (unless and until one author disclaims his ownership interest, as your client apparently has done). You also misstated the facts insomuch as you claimed Mr. Baldwin was not a founder of FIND ME.

In their July 14, 2015 email to Mr. Baldwin, your client further stated Mr. Baldwin was removed as a Board member and regular member because the Board decided he violated all five codes of ethics by falsely stating he was a founding member of FIND ME. The incorporation documents filed with the Arizona Corporation Commission in 2011 that your client personally filed and executed reflects that Mr. Baldwin was in fact a founding Board member of FIND ME, which makes him a *"de facto"* founding member of FIND ME. As a founding Board member, Mr. Baldwin is free to represent this fact. To the extent that your client knowingly utilized the false allegations in your demand letter to mislead the public, create a false light and defame Mr. Baldwin, we will hold them responsible for any resultant damages and injuries.

We demand that you and your client send a retraction letter to all members of FIND ME, including Denise Goodwin Pace of Looking Productions, the Board of Arizona Search Track and Rescue, Cynthia Cannell Literary Agency in New York and any other necessary persons or entities stating that you made a mistake and Mr. Baldwin DID NOT engage in copyright infringement , nor did he violate the five codes of ethics because he was in fact a founding member of FIND ME. If you and your client fail to send a written retraction to the aforesaid recipients by July 28, 2016, we will move forward with our rights and remedies.

Continued on next page

Ms. Crimi Speth, Esq.
July 5, 2016
Page 2.

Your client also violated the Arizona Corporation Code and Internal Revenue Code regarding mandatory disclosure of various corporate documents since Mr. Baldwin requested disclosure in writing on several occasions. As a nonprofit, tax-exempt corporation, your client is required by both state and federal law to disclose various corporate documents upon request and open them for public inspection. Despite demand, your client failed to do so. We are also quite sure your client violated both state and federal notice provisions governing nonprofit, tax-exempt corporations in the way Mr. Baldwin was treated and terminated from the Board.

Should your client fail to remedy these issues by July 28, 2016, we will have no other alternative but move forward with all speed and diligence. Please direct all further discussions through this office.

Respectfully,

Gary A. Wolf

GAW/ac
cc: Client

Appendix 10

My role as a founder of the organization was recognized by Find Me at least as early as 2009.

---

16   **FIND ME**

such as Find Me, and do their best to serve their fellow humans.

One case the psychic and Dan worked that year provides an important lesson for intuitive investigators. A young girl had gone missing in far south Texas. As they attempted to find her, Dan used his pendulum and a process of elimination of locations to zero in on the girl's position. The psychic used her Tarot cards and worked with her spirit guides to get similar information.

As he was closing in, Dan asked an important question. "Is finding this girl in her best interest? Is this effort for the greatest good?" His pendulum began a strong swing toward the "no" position.

Dan backed out of the case and filed no more reports. The psychic's subsequent investigation led to the same conclusion. Although they had found the girl at a specific location, both investigators agreed that sometimes it's in the "missing" person's best interest to remain missing.

"Is taking on this case for the highest good? That's a basic question and one that should be asked before you begin any investigative work," says Dan.

If you haven't guessed by now, this psychic was the same person working with Kelly to found what would become Find Me. Dan was asked to join, and he became the third member of the group.

Find Me now consists of some twenty individuals in the United States, Britain, Italy, Canada and Australia. They are a diverse group, coming from different backgrounds and with different skills and gifts. Many members have contributed to this book. They've all given time, effort, heart and soul to finding missing people, solving crimes and even working to track down criminals and prevent crimes.

Every member doesn't work on every case. Personal schedules, personal interests, involvement in other cases, and, for some, a need to be "called" to a case often dictates who can

Continued on next page

Publisher's Note

FIND ME: How a Unique Group of Psychics, Retired Law Enforcement Officers, and Canine Search and Rescue Volunteers from Around the World Have Banded Together to Find Missing People Copyright ©2007 by Dan Baldwin and Jerry "Kelly" Snyder. All rights reserved. Printed in the United States of America. No part of this book may be used or reproduced in any manner whatsoever without the written permission of the publisher, except in the case of brief quotations. For information, address New River Press, 645 Fairmount Street, Woonsocket, R.I. 02895, (800) 244-1257, books@newriverpress.com

New River Press Web site is: www.newriverpress.com
Book Web site is: www.findmebook.com

Cover by Gary Cascio

FIRST EDITION

Library of Congress Control Number: 2006938361

ISBN: 1-891724-09-6
ISBN 13: 978-1-891724-09-1

Appendix 11

Appendix 12

"During my thirty-five years of work in both the public and private sectors, I have made use of psychic resources on hundreds of investigations. Overall, my success in locating missing individuals has improved dramatically since first using a psychic resource in 1985."
Stephen C. Kopp
Retired Law Enforcement Officer and Private Investigator

"If you are interested in developing your psychic abilities, in helping others, and in serving a higher calling, then I recommend Find Me."
Sonia Choquette
Best-selling author of *Trust Your Vibes*

FIND ME

The Authors:
Dan Baldwin; Dave Campbell, PhD; Stephen D. Earhart; Loretta Greazzo; Jeanette Healey, RN; Sunny Dawn Johnston; Nancy Marlow, BA; Joanne Miller; Eileen Nelson; Chris Robinson; Amanda Schell; Kelly Snyder; and Mary Surrena.

 Dan Baldwin is an author, co-author and ghostwriter of more than 40 business books and his Western novels Trapp Canyon and the Caldera series. He is a founding member of Find Me who often participates in "ground pounding" with the group's sister organization, Arizona Search, Track and Rescue (AZ-STAR).

When Kelly Snyder saw a need for aggressive efforts to find missing persons he founded Find Me to support the efforts of law enforcement and to provide closure to families and individuals affected by the loss of a friend or member of the family. He is a career law enforcement officer with experience in the U.S. Customs Service and the Drug Enforcement Administration.

ISBN 9781475142952

90000 >

9 781475 142952

Appendix 13

This promotion for the radio interview appeared in 2013. Nothing was ever said to me about the reference to being a co-creator with Snyder of Find Me. I was never asked to alter the reference to "inaugural member" or any other such designation.

SUPERNATURAL GIRLZ RADIO
presents Kelly Snyder & Dan Baldwin founders of
FIND ME
Sat, April 6, 9 - 11 pm eastern
FIND MISSING LOVED ONES

Click here to listen LIVE
Use this link to listen to the
FREE archive after the show!

Kelley Snyder is a former law enforcement official who, along with Dan Baldwin created an all volunteer panel of psychic mediums and active law enforcement. They donate their time to finding missing people. Listen to their fascinating story and the incredible nationwide case they're working on now!

Appendix 14

A draft of a query letter to potential publishers. I e-mailed this to Snyder for comment. Note the statement, "I am a co-founder...." Nothing was said to me about refraining from using this reference.

Dan Baldwin

From:	"Dan Baldwin" <baldco1@msn.com>
To:	"kelly snyder" <kilomonster1@gmail.com>
Sent:	Friday, June 19, 2015 6:55 AM
Subject:	Re:

I would be concerned that an agent invests so much energy in trying to obtain a set of rights that are already under contract with another entity. Keep in mind that the agent works for the author - not the other way around.

I still need your comments on the new chapters, but you will have to make time to get those to me. If you want we can do that by telephone interview. It shouldn't take a long time.

Here's the query letter for *Find Me - The Casebook*. If you can think of something to add that will jazz it up, plug that in and send it back to me asap.

Again, thanks for the kind words for *The Practical Pendulum*. A signed copy is headed your way by snail mail.

Dan

Dear _____,

If you could increase your chances of finding a missing loved one, catching a murderer or kidnapper, or solving a cold case by 50 percent or more, would you take that chance?

Find Me is an international volunteer organization that provides that 50 percent or better chance. The group is composed of 200 vetted psychics, retired and active law enforcement personnel, and trained forensic and investigative professionals dedicated to finding missing persons and solving crimes. Find Me has provided services to legal authorities throughout the United States and in Canada, Mexico, Ireland, Italy, and Japan. Active supporters of the group include actor Bruce Willis, advertising legend Mary Wells Lawrence, and law enforcement agencies that regularly call on the group for assistance.

Find Me – The Case Book relates 18 cases, including investigations of serial killings, mysterious disappearances, and unexplained deaths. Several chapters involve hazardous on-the-scene investigations with a sister group Arizona Search Track and Rescue. Chapters also highlight the history of Find Me and offer guidelines for founding a psychic detecting group.

Find Me was founded in 2002 by Kelly Snyder, a retired federal agent with more than 25 years of experience in the Drug Enforcement Agency. I am a co-founder of the group. I am a ghostwriter, co-author or author of more than 50 books on business and related topics and the author of five Western

Appendix 15

May 16, 2016

Mr. Kelly Snyder
2770 E. Buena Vista Drive
Chandler, AZ 85249

Ms. Sunny Dawn Johnson
4634 Redfield Road
Glendale, AZ 85306

Mr. Dave Campbell
THE ASTROLOGY STORE
5735 West Glendale Ave.
Glendale, AZ 85301

Board of Directors-Find Me
Via Email only:
Kileymaster@gmail.com
sundown@cox.net
theastrologystore@gmail.com
jwdenberg@yahoo.com
conlinunter@seanet.com
nra.mune@gmail.com

RE: Mr. Dan Baldwin

Ladies and Gentlemen:

I am in receipt of Mr. Snyder's email letter regarding Mr. Baldwin's request to rescind his termination from your records and thus reinstating him onto the Board of Directors of Find Me. Immediately upon the reinstatement, Mr. Baldwin is prepared to submit the enclosed resignation. The Board can then accept the resignation.

Mr. Baldwin, at my suggestion, believes that the Board can correct the minutes by stating "Dan Baldwin was not in violation of the Find Me code of ethics and has been reinstated as a member in good standing to the Board of Directors." In this way, the record is clear, concise and correct.

459 N. Granada Avenue
Tucson, Arizona 85701
tom@mediationoftucson.com

520.622.4622 (Ph)
520.882.9861 (Fax)

Continued on next page

Page 2
Letter Dated 5/16/2016
Baldwin/Find Me

So that everyone is on board, Mr. Baldwin and the Board of Directors can agree as follows:

1. Find Me will reinstate Mr. Baldwin as a member and Board Member in good standing;

2. The Board of Directors' action reinstating Mr. Baldwin will be entered into the official minutes;

3. Mr. Baldwin will execute and tender his resignation in writing.

4. Each member of Find Me will be notified of Mr. Baldwin's reinstatement in good standing in a message separate from the minutes;

5. The Board of Directors of Arizona Search Track and Rescue (AZ-STAR) will be notified both of the reinstatement and subsequent resignation;

6. Denise Goodwin Pace of Looking Productions will be notified both of the reinstatement and subsequent resignation;

7. Maria Crimi Speth of Jaburg-Wilkes Attorneys at Law will be notified both of the reinstatement and subsequent resignation; and

8. Mr. Baldwin will not discuss or make any disparaging remarks about the organization and the organization will act likewise toward him.

I have enclosed an unsigned copy of the purposed resignation and agreement from Mr. Baldwin. I have asked him to execute it and return it to me so that I in turn can forward it to each of you upon completion of this transaction.

I also want to take this opportunity to thank Mr. Baldwin and each of you for resolving this issue using alternative dispute resolution.

So that we can have this completed and finalized by the end of this month, may I suggest that you do what is necessary in order to re-instate Mr. Baldwin and correct the record and Mr. Baldwin, you execute the letter of resignation and return it to me so I can forward it to the Find Me organization. I would like to

Continued on next page

Page 3
Letter Dated 5/16/2016
Baldwin/Find Me

have everything in hand no later than Friday May 27, 2016. So that this transaction is completed by Tuesday May 31, 2016.

If any individual or entity has a question, please let me know.

Thank you.

Sincerely,

Thomas T. Tilton
Mediation of Tucson

TTT/mm
cc: Mr. Dan Baldwin
Enclosure

Appendix 16

Dan Baldwin

From: "kelly snyder" <kilomonster1@gmail.com>
To: "Dan" <baldco@msn.com>
Sent: Monday, July 6, 2015 8:34 AM
Subject: Find Me Group

Dan,

Friendship aside, I need to discuss two things that have been bothering me for quite some time. You have been telling people and recently put into print on your book stating you are a co-founder of Find Me. You are not a co-founder. You are a inaugural member and board member. That would be an accurate and appropriate statement and one I am happy to support.

You must remove this statement from your book immediately.

There also needs to be clarity about my book and its content. I want to remind you how the start of book two unfolded.

I decided in 2011 to write another book, but 100% in my style of writing. Later that year or in early 2012 you asked if I was considering writing another book. I stated at that time I was considering it, but again repeated that it was going to be in my style. You stated " if you need or want my help I would be glad to help you."

With that said, I stated I would someday figure out the direction of the book. Co-authorship was never mentioned. You agreed to help me, but now I am getting the distinct impression you see yourself as co-author. I cannot have a co-author since my contract with Denise would not allow it. I allowed you to assist me and planned on sharing in the proceeds with you, but that is as far as it would go with your involvement. I am happy to pay you an appropriate fee for the work you have done on the book as soon as the book is sold you will receive compensation and I am happy to put this in writing.

You stated in our last conversation that you went ahead and did a copy-write procedure on the book. I am troubled by this statement as I didn't ask you to do this. It is an unnecessary step as my agent and publisher will handle this. More importantly, did you make Find Me or myself as owner? If you did not, then this needs to be corrected immediately.

I need you to honor this arrangement by taking the necessary steps to correct the above mentioned items. I will move forward with you in a clear and cohesive manner and we can also discuss this, but the last time we spoke you were less than cooperative.

I appreciate all that you have done for myself and Find Me and would like to continue our friendship and your valued role as a trusted Find Me member.

Kelly

Appendix 17

The Baldwin/Snyder copyright was initiated in 2009 and remained in force until Snyder demanded to be removed as an author or co-author.

Find Me, Too

(Working Title)

© Dan Baldwin/Kelly Snyder 2009

Appendix 18

Although Snyder claims the Find Me book wasn't begun until 2011 or later, he was shopping it to an agent in 2010. As the e-mails show, the project was well underway well before 2011.

Dan Baldwin

From:	"Kelly" <kilomonster@cox.net>
To:	"'Dan Baldwin'" <baldco@msn.com>
Sent:	Thursday, January 21, 2010 8:45 AM
Subject:	RE: FINDTWO1A

I filled them in and read the entire thing one more time. I would assume she will consider that it is a work in progress.. I also made the spelling and grammar corrections.. I also told her that when we talked. she said send it regardless.. so I doubt she will be critical of anything except our content. but since we are perfect. that shouldn't be an issue either..

From: Dan Baldwin [mailto:baldco@msn.com]
Sent: Thursday, January 21, 2010 8:11 AM
To: Kelly
Subject: Re: FINDTWO1A

Agh!

It needs a final read-through on this end unless you've already done that.
There are those holes you need to fill I mentioned.
Nothing major, but it hasn't been thoroughly proofed.

Dan

> ----- Original Message -----
> **From:** Kelly
> **To:** cannell@cannellagency.com
> **Sent:** Thursday, January 21, 2010 7:42 AM
> **Subject:** FINDTWO1A

Cynthia,

Great talking with you . attached are chapters we have completed so far.

The idea behind the book is to provide cases we have worked on that were successful & our failures with a common theme that the psychic phenomenon is real, but there needs to be improvement. we have research projects ongoing to highlight our efforts to improve the psychic abilities. Those projects will be explained in one of our chapters.

We are also bringing to the table handwriting experts, face readers, interviewing experts, retired FBI profiler, body language experts, voice analysis experts, and a list of technical equipment that I will send you later. The book will cover every aspect of what is necessary to cover every base of conducting a search.. investigative, technical, and with the psychic element as the keynote component that the police need to incorporate in their arsenal of investigative tools. we want to close the gap on missing person and homicide cases for law enforcement.

Thanks for taking a look..

Kelly

No virus found in this incoming message.
Checked by AVG - www.avg.com
Version: 9.0.730 / Virus Database: 271.1.1/2635 - Release Date: 01/20/10 12:18:00

Continued on next page

Dan Baldwin

From: "Kelly Snyder" <kilomonster@cox.net>
To: "Dan" <baldco@msn.com>
Sent: Wednesday, January 02, 2013 9:41 AM
Subject: FW: following up on your book (per Peggy Rometo)

FYI...

From: Kelly Snyder [mailto:kilomonster@cox.net]
Sent: Wednesday, January 02, 2013 9:41 AM
To: 'Cynthia Cannell'
Subject: RE: following up on your book (per Peggy Rometo)

It should be finalized somewhere in the month of February or sooner... We currently have ten chapters done and intend on at least 15 chapters.. Thanks again for your interest and I will keep in touch with you.

Kelly

From: Cynthia Cannell [mailto:cannell@cannellagency.com]
Sent: Wednesday, January 02, 2013 9:11 AM
To: kilomonster@cox.net
Subject: following up on your book (per Peggy Rometo)

Kelly,

Peggy told me you're making progress on your new book -- I'd be pleased to review it and talk to you about it, at your convenience.

Best wishes for the New Year!

Cynthia

Cynthia Cannell
Cynthia Cannell Literary Agency
833 Madison Avenue
New York, New York 10021
p: +1 212 396 9595
f: +1 212 396 9797

cannellagency.com

Continued on next page

Dan Baldwin

From:	"Dan Baldwin" <baldco@msn.com>
To:	<cannell@cannellagency.com>
Cc:	"Kelly Snyder" <kilomonster1@gmail.com>
Sent:	Saturday, February 21, 2015 3:53 PM
Attach:	FINDTWOREV.docx
Subject:	FIND ME MANUSCRIPT RE: KELLY SNYDER

Dan Baldwin
480-807-9682
baldco@msn.com
www.fourknightspress.com www.danbaldwin.biz

Cynthia,

Attached is the unfinished manuscript for the FIND ME followup book for your review.

We recently gutted the original to replace about half the chapters which were interesting, but with undetermined or unsuccessful outcomes.

We're replacing them with successful cases.

PLEASE NOTE:

Four of the seven new chapters have been written, but have not been proofed for grammar, spelling or "omph." Three chapters are yet to be written, but will be in rough draft form by no later than the first week in March. They are noted in bold in the TOC.

These seven chapters require Kelly's insight and commentary and the above mentioned work on my end.

Completion of the manuscript will be a priority upon Kelly's return from his overseas trip.

All comments are most welcome. If you have any questions at all please call or e-mail.

Thanks.

Dan

Continued on next page

Dan Baldwin

From:	"Dan Baldwin" <baldco@msn.com>
To:	"kelly snyder" <kilomonster1@gmail.com>
Sent:	Monday, April 13, 2015 4:31 AM
Subject:	Re: Jury finds Randy Taylor guilty of Alexis Murphy's murder	WTVR.com

We tossed out half our book and I rewrote an entire new half based on her recommendation. She owes us
the basic business courtesy of a quick response.

I'll start the rewrite on the new chapters today and will wrap by the end of the week. All we'll need then
is your comments on the new chapters.

We've already written Find Me II. There's no way you can do it on your own. No matter how you look at
it, she is talking about an entirely separate book. I say go for it, but this one is basically ready to go.

For a number of sound reasons we need to get this book into the marketplace now.

Dan

> ----- Original Message -----
> From: kelly snyder
> To: Dan
> Sent: Sunday, April 12, 2015 12:50 PM
> Subject: Fwd: Jury finds Randy Taylor guilty of Alexis Murphy's murder | WTVR.com
>
>
> Begin forwarded message:
>
>> From: "Dan Baldwin" <baldco@msn.com>
>> Subject: Re: Jury finds Randy Taylor guilty of Alexis Murphy's murder |
>> WTVR.com
>> Date: April 12, 2015 at 12:06:35 PM MST
>> To: "kelly snyder" <kilomonster1@gmail.com>
>>
>> Good deal.
>>
>> In other news, I'd like to wrap the book up in April. I can driver over
>> to your place for an interview on the
>> remaining chapters (found a Cuban cigar maker in your neighborhood)
>> or we could do that by phone -
>> whatever is easiest on you. I am waiting for a response from Cynthia
>> which should give me some direction... nothing has changed.,.. she
>> wants me to do the book on my own and I am doing my best to figure
>> you into this equation !!
>>
>> Also, please and por favor, I started my once and future pendulum
>> quide book this month and will finish

Appendix 19

This is an e-mail showing that Snyder was working with me on the book in 2010. Note also, that seven chapters had been completed by this time and I was about to start writing on the eighth. Notice also who is doing the actual writing.

Dan Baldwin

From: "Kelly" <kilomonster@cox.net>
To: "'Dan Baldwin'" <baldco@msn.com>
Sent: Wednesday, October 27, 2010 2:01 PM
Subject: RE:
One with Melissa Frei on her sister Lisa Bouellert or something like that...

From: Dan Baldwin [mailto:baldco@msn.com]
Sent: Wednesday, October 27, 2010 8:12 AM
To: Kelly
Subject: Re:

Okay.
Sheddy on hold.
Do we have other similar cases where only volunteers from the group were involved?
Anyway, send me notes on another chapter ASAP and let's push this thing on through
as far as we can.
I think there's going to be a lot of interest next year.

Any illegal alien with a gold mine es mi amigo grande!

----- Original Message -----
From: Kelly
To: 'Dan Baldwin'
Sent: Wednesday, October 27, 2010 8:03 AM
Subject: RE:

I would suggest that we either do three or four cases like Sheddy in one chapter or NOT at all. I have
zero on the case and it is not a case I assigned to the group.

I already notified Kristi and she said to take her quote and write it the way she said it in the interview
and she would acknowledge she said it..... Or send her the quote and she would rewrite it for you in
an email....

Lost Dutchman is an illegal alien.....

From: Dan Baldwin [mailto:baldco@msn.com]
Sent: Wednesday, October 27, 2010 7:23 AM
To: Kelly Snyder
Subject:

Kelly,

Attached is the complete new manuscript with the Stover chapter added. We will need to
really
go over this one in the final draft as we are writing about future events now that will be
past
events by publication.

I'll start on Christine Sheddy as chapter eight, an example of individual members
volunteering
their time and efforts. I have the basic story from news accounts. Please forward any of
our

Appendix 20

Snyder's reply (embedded in my e-mail) states that agent Cannell wants Snyder to write the book on his own. This is the first instance in which *our* book begins to shift toward *his* book.

backed by scientific data, complimented by intelligence analysts and investigative expertise/experience and presented to law enforcement agencies as leads to solve those crimes and locate missing people.

The ultimate goal of Find Me has always been to find people that have gone missing....and we want to find them alive. Unfortunately, this is not always the case, but if foul play is suspected or identified to then be able to assist law enforcement in solving the crime, bringing the suspects to justice and bring closure to families and law enforcement.

Find Me is also being requested to look into cases of human trafficking and of course we are considering taking on this challenge, since it is a natural progression of locating missing people that have been kidnapped and forced into a life of crime. We want to take on all new challenges, but also not lose focus of our main goals and also not spread our efforts so thin we lose control and diminish our success.

The psychic phenomena is real and does exist. We are doing research, testing, and creating ways to perfect the psychics abilities to become more accurate and striving for the end result to be in the 80%-90% accuracy range. When a person goes missing and there is no evidence or leads to identify where this person may have gone, then where do you start to look.? Utilizing the various skills of psychics narrows the gap and provides leads of where to start looking. This by it's simple nature clears the areas where at least we now know the missing person is not where we have looked. In some missing person investigations the psychics have identified an area where we discovered the missing person and we were as close as one foot from the exact location. This is considered impossible by the skeptics, but in reality has happened on numerous occasions with the Find Me Team. We want law enforcement to utilize our techniques from the very start of an investigation. We can provide leads and given the opportunity can follow up on certain leads ourselves to assist in the process, by always helping and not hindering the investigation. Immediate response by the canine partners is also essential to be on scene immediately to locate the scent and follow it to the missing person if circumstances and gathered facts allows this procedure to be utilized.

Bottom line is Find Me is here to help and will not interfere with law enforcement but compliment their investigation and in most cases assist them in locating the missing person immediately, if given the chance. Being requested two days, two weeks, two months or two years to assist does not change our accuracy , but may change the outcome of finding the person deceased instead of being alive. All we ask is to be given a chance and we promise to give it our best and the history of our success validates this unique process.

I will most likely expand this or work on it a little more, but feel free to add, delete or make it prettier....

Appendix 21

The reference here is to "the" book and not a "new" book or "different" book.

Subject: Re: Jury finds Randy Taylor guilty of Alexis Murphy's murder | WTVR.com
Date: April 12, 2015 at 12:06:35 PM MST
To: "kelly snyder" <kilomonster1@gmail.com>

Good deal.

In other news, I'd like to wrap the book up in April. I can driver over to your place for an interview on the remaining chapters (found a Cuban cigar maker in your neighborhood) or we could do that by phone - whatever is easiest on you. I am waiting for a response from Cynthia which should give me some direction... nothing has changed.,.. she wants me to do the book on my own and I am doing my best to figure you into this equation !!

Also, please and por favor, I started my once and future pendulum guide book this month and will finish that within a week or so. Consider writing a cover blurb for me on that, you know, something along the lines of best thing since bottled bread and sliced beer. I'll send you a copy of the manuscript, of course. Glad to say some words of wisdom...!!

Dan'l

----- Original Message -----
From: kelly snyder
To: Dan
Sent: Sunday, April 12, 2015 11:50 AM
Subject: Re: Jury finds Randy Taylor guilty of Alexis Murphy's murder | WTVR.com

They found her hair in his trailer and I believe he is also the main suspect in Samantha Clark....... may be going there to search with NBC crew..... waiting for an answer from police...

On Apr 12, 2015, at 11:48 AM, Dan Baldwin <baldco@msn.com> wrote:

Curious that I got he was involved, but not the killer.
Doesn't add up with the .

Continued on next page

Dan Baldwin

From:	"kelly snyder" <kilomonster1@gmail.com>
To:	"Dan" <baldco@msn.com>
Sent:	Monday, April 13, 2015 7:06 AM
Subject:	Fwd: Jury finds Randy Taylor guilty of Alexis Murphy's murder	WTVR.com

Begin forwarded message:

> **From:** "Dan Baldwin" <baldco@msn.com>
> **Subject: Re: Jury finds Randy Taylor guilty of Alexis Murphy's murder | WTVR.com**
> **Date:** April 13, 2015 at 4:31:58 AM MST
> **To:** "kelly snyder" <kilomonster1@gmail.com>
>
> We tossed out half our book and I rewrote an entire new half based on her recommendation. She owes us
> the basic business courtesy of a quick response. Rewrote what ... not sure I know what you are referring to..?   The only changes recommended were initially from Joni..!!
>
> I'll start the rewrite on the new chapters today and will wrap by the end of the week. All we'll need then
> is your comments on the new chapters. Hold off until I can sort this out.....
>
> We've already written Find Me II. There's no way you can do it on your own. No matter how you look at
> it, she is talking about an entirely separate book. I say go for it, but this one is basically ready to go.
>
> For a number of sound reasons we need to get this book into the marketplace now. She is currently out of the country and returns on the 23rd.... she wants to talk then, so stand by until then...
>
> Dan
>
> > ----- Original Message -----
> > **From:** kelly snyder
> > **To:** Dan
> > **Sent:** Sunday, April 12, 2015 12:50 PM
> > **Subject:** Fwd: Jury finds Randy Taylor guilty of Alexis Murphy's murder | WTVR.com
> >
> > Begin forwarded message:
> >
> > > From: "Dan Baldwin" <baldco@msn.com>

Continued on next page

Dan Baldwin

From:	"Dan Baldwin" <baldco@centurylink.net>
To:	<baldco@msn.com>
Sent:	Monday, July 27, 2015 12:57 PM
Subject:	Fwd: Co-Founder reverence

From: "kelly snyder" <kilomonster1@gmail.com>
To: "Dan Baldwin" <baldco@centurylink.net>
Sent: Friday, July 17, 2015 11:52:41 AM
Subject: Fwd: Co-Founder reverence

Begin forwarded message:

From: Dan Baldwin <baldco@centurylink.net>
Subject: Re: Co-Founder reverence
Date: July 17, 2015 at 9:42:36 AM MST
To: kelly snyder <kilomonster1@gmail.com>, sunnydawn@cox.net,
theastrologystore@gmail.com, jwdenboer@yahoo.com,
quailhunter@seanet.com, peg.rometo@gmail.com, baldco@msn.com

Kelly,
I continue in response to comments coming my way.

The e-mail you sent to me and the board yesterday addressed my "lack of
truthfulness." In that e-mail you stated unambiguously "I have personally "never"
heard you use the that term co-founder in my presence." Your e-mail to me of
July 8, 2015 says just the opposite. "For the record I have only heard you make
that reference in recent months." I wanted the board to be aware of this
contradiction. That reference is from NYC event… how much more clearer can I make
this..??

As to the book (working title Find Me Two): As promised I will forward a
clarification to the board today.

Also, your e-mail to me July 14, 2015 states that "I do not want any part or
portion of the book..." I take you at your word on that. Itâ€™s yours to keep, just make

Continued on next page

comments are in the bookâ€¦. Find Me name cannot be made reference to either or that this is sanctioned by Find Me. My attorney will be sending you a confirmation of all of this, so that there are NO misunderstandings...

As always, I am available to any board member to answer any questions Final emailâ€¦ it is now in the hands of attorneys and youâ€¦..
about this matter.

Dan

From: "kelly snyder" <kilomonster1@gmail.com>
To: "Dan Baldwin" <baldco@centurylink.net>
Sent: Friday, July 17, 2015 8:35:00 AM
Subject: Re: Co-Founder reverence

It refers to the NYC eventâ€¦. why keep up this diatribe when it is obvious you are reaching for anything to take the focus off of youâ€¦.

We will now wait to see what your move is about the bookâ€¦.

On Jul 16, 2015, at 2:36 PM, Dan Baldwin <baldco@centurylink.net>
wrote:

Kelly,

Regarding truthfulness:

Your statement to the board of directors of Find Me about you never hearing
me use the term "co-founder"
in your presence is, as you know, false.

This is the line cut directly from your e-mail:

Appendix 22

Somehow AZSTAR was brought into the matter. Notice how the President of AZSTAR followed the CEO of Find Me in attempting to assert a non-existent right of censorship of matters concerning their organizations.

July 12, 2015

Dan Baldwin
6311 E. Regina
Mesa, AZ 85215

Mr. Baldwin:

You are in possession of written information, pictures and other data, including but not limited to, a chapter for a book that was provided to Kelly Snyder of Find Me for inclusion in the book being authored by Kelly Snyder about Find Me and the work that the organization does.

Arizona Search Track and Rescue, Inc. (AZ STaR) does not now nor has ever conveyed to Dan Baldwin permission to utilize this information (pictures, emails, written word or any other data) and furthermore Arizona Search Track and Rescue does not convey in any way shape or form, any permissions to Dan Baldwin to utilize any information (pictures, emails, written word or any other data) about AZ STaR and/or any information relative to any search & rescue missions that Arizona Search Track and Rescue, Inc. has been involved with.

Should you have any questions regarding this request, please direct it to:

> Gregory Robinson,
> Attorney at Law
> Farley, Robinson, & Larsen
> 6040 N. Seventh Street
> Suite #300
> Phoenix, AZ 85014-1803

Sincerely,

Kristi Smith
President
Arizona Search Track and Rescue, Inc.

Cc: Kelly Snider, Find Me
        Denise Goodwin Pace, Looking Up Productions

Arizona Search Track and Rescue, Inc.
P.O. Box 5535
Peoria, AZ 85385-5535
Phone: 623-878-9149 emergencies: 888-307-3709 Fax: 623-271-8137

Appendix 23

Note the subject line: copyright infringement.

3200 N. CENTRAL AVENUE, 20TH FLOOR, PHOENIX, AZ 85012

jaburgwilk.com

JABURG|WILK
Attorneys at Law

Maria Crimi Speth

mcs@jaburgwilk.com
602.248.1089 – Direct Phone
602.248.0522 – Main Fax

July 29, 2015

Via E-Mail: baldco1@msn.com
               baldco@msn.com
               baldco@centurylink.net
and U. S. Mail

Gary J. Jaburg
Lawrence E. Wilk
Roger L. Cohen
Mitchell Reichman
Beth S. Cohn
Kraig J. Marton
Ronald M. Horwitz
Maria Crimi Speth
Neal H. Bookspan
Kathi M. Sandweiss
Mervyn T. Braude
Lauren L. Garner
Michelle C. Lombino
Janessa E. Koenig
Mark D. Bogard
David N. Farren
David L. Allen
Laurence B. Hirsch
Jennifer R. Erickson
Nathan D. Meyer
Jason B. Castle
Douglas O. Guffey
C. Cole Crabtree
Erick S. Durlach
Thomas S. Moring
Matthew T. Anderson
Laura A. Rogal
Amy M. Horwitz
Nichole H. Wilk
Jeffrey A. Silence
Shawdy Banihashemi
Aaron K. Haar

Dan Baldwin
6311 E. Regina St.
Mesa, AZ 85215

   Re: Copyright Infringement -- Find Me

Dear Mr. Baldwin:

   This firm represents Kelly Snyder and Find Me, Inc. in connection with the protection and enforcement of their intellectual property rights. I understand that you and Mr. Snyder had been working together over the past three-and-a-half years to co-author a book about the Find Me group. I also understand that the two of you ultimately parted ways. You have since claimed that you "copyrighted" the book, including Mr. Snyder's portion, and that you intend to move forward with publishing the book on your own. I also understand that you have previously incorrectly represented yourself as a co-founder of Find Me.

   The purpose of this letter is two-fold: (1) to demand that you not use Mr. Snyder's copyright-protected work; and (2) to demand that you immediately cease using the trademark FIND ME in any way that suggests sponsorship, endorsement, or affiliation with you or your work.

   <u>Mr. Snyder's Writings</u>

   Regardless of any action you may have taken to register the copyright in the planned book, Mr. Snyder retains the copyrights in the material he created/authored. Copyrights in a given work automatically vest in the author of the work. *See* 17 U.S.C. § 201(a). Mr. Snyder independently authored 17 of the chapters in the draft of the book. Mr. Snyder also created various audio recordings in connection with the book, for which he similarly retains copyrights. Mr. Snyder's copyrights in these works are exclusive rights under the Copyright Act, 17 U.S.C. § 106.

Continued on next page

JABURG|WILK
Attorneys at Law
Dan Baldwin
July 29, 2015
Page 2

For you to have any claim to these chapters and audio recordings, Mr. Snyder would have had to affirmatively assign his rights in the works to you. An assignment of copyright must be in writing pursuant to 17 U.S.C. § 204(a) and must be clear and unequivocal. *The Weinstein Company v. Smokewood Entertainment Group, LLC*, 664 F. Supp. 2d 332, 340 (S.D.N.Y. 2009). Indeed, the very purpose of §204(a) is that it "ensures that the creator of a work will not give away his copyright inadvertently and forces a party who wants to use the copyrighted work to negotiate with the creator to determine precisely what rights are being transferred and at what price." *Effects Assoc., Inc. v. Cohen*, 908 F.2d 555, 557 (9th Cir.1990); *see Konigsberg Int'l, Inc.*, 16 F.3d 355, 357 (9th Cir. 1994). Moreover, "§ 204(a)'s writing requirement not only protects authors from fraudulent claims, but also enhances predictability and certainty of ownership—Congress's paramount goal when it revised the Act in 1976." *Id.* (internal citations omitted); see also *Schiller & Schmidt, Inc. v. Nordisco Corp.*, 969 F.2d 410, 412 (7th Cir. 1992) (holding that [17 U.S.C.] § 101's requirements of a written statement for copyright ownership of works for hire "is not merely a statute of frauds"; it is also intended "to make the ownership of property rights in intellectual property clear and definite, so that such property will be readily marketable"). Since Mr. Snyder has not executed any such assignment, it is undisputed that he retains exclusive ownership of the copyrights in the portions of the book that he wrote.

Moreover, it is copyright infringement to copy a work in its entirety, or to copy constituent elements of the work that are original. *Feist Publications, Inc. v. Rural Telephone Service Co., Inc.*, 499 U.S. 340, 361, 111 S.Ct. 1282, 113 L.Ed.2d 358 (1991). Thus, you may not use Mr. Snyder's authored works even if you make changes or revisions to it. To the extent you take and use any of that work, or adopt that work in similar form, you will be liable for copyright infringement. Such action would constitute a willful infringement of my client's copyrights, which would entitle Mr. Snyder to recover the damages and obtain injunctive relief. *See* 17 U.S.C. § 504–505.

Moreover, the Copyright Act makes it a federal crime to willfully infringe ones copyrights for commercial advantage or private financial gain. 17 U.S.C. § 506(a). Making a false representation of a material fact—such as claims of ownership—in a copyright registration also constitutes a federal crime. *See id.* § 506(e). Therefore, you are advised that any actions you take, or have taken, to use or register my client's works will subject you to both civil and criminal liability.

The FIND ME Trademark

The Find Me organization maintains exclusive right to use the trademark FIND ME in connection with missing persons investigations. This mark has been used in commerce continually since 2003. The mark is registered with the United States Patent and Trademark Office under Registration No. 4427655.

The "core element" of trademark infringement law is whether an alleged trademark infringer's use of a mark creates a likelihood of confusion as to who is behind the product. *See Brother Records, Inc. v. Jardine*, 318 F.3d 900, 908 (9th Cir. 2003). Any false assertion or implication of sponsorship, endorsement, or affiliation constitutes trademark infringement. *See Mattel, Inc. v. Walking Mountain Productions*, 353 F.3d 792, 806–807, 69 U.S.P.Q.2d 1257 (9th Cir. 2003) ("Generally, to assess whether a defendant has infringed on a plaintiff's trademark, we apply a 'likelihood of confusion' test that asks whether use of the plaintiff's trademark by the defendant is 'likely to cause confusion or to cause

Continued on next page

105

JABURG|WILK
Attorneys at Law
Dan Baldwin
July 29, 2015
Page 3

mistake, or to deceive as to the affiliation, connection, or association' of the two products."). Given that any book you publish will directly compete with any book actually sanctioned by Find Me, the likelihood of confusion is quite high. *See AMF Inc. v. Sleekcraft Boats*, 599 F.2d 341, 348 (9th Cir. 1979) ("When the goods produced by the alleged infringer compete for sales with those of the trademark owner, infringement usually will be found if the marks are sufficiently similar that confusion can be expected."). Federal statutes provide for civil remedies for infringement of a trademark, including damages, costs, and attorney fees. 15 U.S.C. § 1114.

Thus, to the extent you choose to move forward with publishing your original writings, you may not use the trademark FIND ME in any way that suggests sponsorship, endorsement, or affiliation with you or with your work. You also may not use Mr. Snyder's name or imply any sponsorship, endorsement, or affiliation with Mr. Snyder. And you may not falsely state or imply that you are a co-founder of Find Me. Moreover, I note that you are currently subject to an agreement with Denise Goodwin Pace that restricts your ability to write about Mr. Snyder without prior written approval. Contract damages may also be available to Ms. Pace if you violate that agreement.

Conclusion

In conclusion, you must refrain from using or registering any of Mr. Snyder's work. To the extent you have already submitted any portion of Mr. Snyder's work for federal copyright registration, you must immediately withdraw the application from consideration. You must also immediately cease using the mark FIND ME in any way that suggests sponsorship, endorsement, or affiliation with you or your work. You also may not use Mr. Snyder's name or imply any sponsorship, endorsement, or affiliation with Mr. Snyder. And you may not falsely state or imply that you are a co-founder of Find Me. Please respond to this letter in writing no later than August 7, 2015 to confirm you will comply with these demands.

Sincerely,

JABURG & WILK, P.C.

Maria Crimi Speth

MCS:akh

Appendix 24

Dan Baldwin

From: "Denise Goodwin Pace" <deniselookingup@aol.com>
To: <kilomonster@cox.net>; <baldco@msn.com>
Sent: Friday, February 01, 2013 11:04 AM
Subject: literary agents

Kelly and Dan

I've spoken to both Terri Wolf (AKA Literary) and Cynthia Cannell (Cynthia Cannell Literary Agency, NYC), like them both, would like to see you two get what you deserve from the next and subsequent books on FindMe.

Because Pounding the Ground is in the works about FindMe, I think it gives you some momentum for a better book deal and I'd like to see you capitalize on that in advance of our TV deal.

Cynthia, today, asked me for you to send what you have done on the second book to her so she can read it over the weekend. She has a lot of authors on her website.

You might do that and then see how you feel about reaching back to Terri to see what she is offering (don't tell one about the other - to Cynthia, I only alluded to the fact that you are now being pursued by several literary agents).

These are your decisions to make, they don't affect me, but I wanted to try to assist, if I can.

Best

Denise

Denise Goodwin Pace
Looking Up Productions
142 Sandy Hollow Road
Northport, NY 11768
631-757-6311
deniselookingup@aol.com

Appendix 25

Although I sent the manuscript and my name appears in the copyright notice with Snyder's name, no one from the Cannell Agency ever contacted me about the project. At this point the conversation apparently becomes a two-way between Snyder and the agent.

Note also that the new chapters mentioned require Snyder's input, input never provided.

Dan Baldwin

From:	"Dan Baldwin" <baldco@msn.com>
To:	<cannell@cannellagency.com>
Cc:	"Kelly Snyder" <kilomonster1@gmail.com>
Sent:	Saturday, February 21, 2015 3:53 PM
Attach:	FINDTWOREV.docx
Subject:	FIND ME MANUSCRIPT RE: KELLY SNYDER

Dan Baldwin
480-807-9682
baldco@msn.com
www.fourknightspress.com www.danbaldwin.biz

Cynthia,

Attached is the unfinished manuscript for the FIND ME followup book for your review.

We recently gutted the original to replace about half the chapters which were interesting, but with undetermined or unsuccessful outcomes.

We're replacing them with successful cases.

PLEASE NOTE:

Four of the seven new chapters have been written, but have not been proofed for grammar, spelling or "omph." Three chapters are yet to be written, but will be in rough draft form by no later than the first week in March. They are noted in bold in the TOC.

These seven chapters require Kelly's insight and commentary and the above mentioned work on my end.

Completion of the manuscript will be a priority upon Kelly's return from his overseas trip.

All comments are most welcome. If you have any questions at all please call or e-mail.

Thanks.

Dan

Appendix 26

I'm not against you writing another book. In fact, I'll be glad to help any
way I can if you want. Like I said, go for it.

This specific little piggy just needs to get to market and soon.

Dan

----- Original Message -----
From: kelly snyder
To: Dan
Sent: Monday, April 13, 2015 7:06 AM
Subject: Fwd: Jury finds Randy Taylor guilty of Alexis Murphy's murder | WTVR.com

Begin forwarded message:

From: "Dan Baldwin" <baldco@msn.com>
Subject: Re: Jury finds Randy Taylor guilty of Alexis Murphy's murder | WTVR.com
Date: April 13, 2015 at 4:31:58 AM MST
To: "kelly snyder" <kilomonster1@gmail.com>

We tossed out half our book and I rewrote an entire new half based on her recommendation. She owes us the basic business courtesy of a quick response. Rewrote what ... not sure I know what you are referring to..? The only changes recommended were initially from Joni..!!

I'll start the rewrite on the new chapters today and will wrap by the end of the week. All we'll need then is your comments on the new chapters. Hold off until I can sort this out.....

We've already written Find Me II. There's no way you can do it on your own. No matter how you look at it, she is talking about an entirely separate book. I say go for it, but this one is basically ready to go.

For a number of sound reasons we need to get this book into the marketplace now. She is currently out of the country and returns on the 23rd.... she wants to talk then, so stand by until then...

Dan

Appendix 27

Dan Baldwin

From:	"kelly snyder" <kilomonster1@gmail.com>
To:	"Dan" <baldco@msn.com>
Sent:	Monday, April 13, 2015 7:06 AM
Subject:	Fwd: Jury finds Randy Taylor guilty of Alexis Murphy's murder	WTVR.com

Begin forwarded message:

> From: "Dan Baldwin" <baldco@msn.com>
> **Subject: Re: Jury finds Randy Taylor guilty of Alexis Murphy's murder |**
> **WTVR.com**
> Date: April 13, 2015 at 4:31:58 AM MST
> To: "kelly snyder" <kilomonster1@gmail.com>
>
> We tossed out half our book and I rewrote an entire new half based on her
> recommendation. She owes us
> the basic business courtesy of a quick response. Rewrote what ... not sure I know
> what you are referring to..?   The only changes recommended were initially from
> Joni..!!
>
> I'll start the rewrite on the new chapters today and will wrap by the end of the
> week. All we'll need then
> is your comments on the new chapters. Hold off until I can sort this out.....
>
> We've already written Find Me II. There's no way you can do it on your own. No
> matter how you look at
> it, she is talking about an entirely separate book. I say go for it, but this one is
> basically ready to go.
>
> For a number of sound reasons we need to get this book into the marketplace
> now. She is currently out of the country and returns on the 23rd.... she wants to
> talk then, so stand by until then...
>
> Dan
>
> > ----- Original Message -----
> > From: kelly snyder
> > To: Dan
> > Sent: Sunday, April 12, 2015 12:50 PM
> > Subject: Fwd: Jury finds Randy Taylor guilty of Alexis Murphy's murder |
> > WTVR.com
> >
> > Begin forwarded message:
> >
> > From: "Dan Baldwin" <baldco@msn.com>

Appendix 28

Dan Baldwin

From:	"Dan Baldwin" <baldco@msn.com>
To:	"kelly snyder" <kilomonster1@gmail.com>
Sent:	Monday, April 13, 2015 11:57 AM
Subject:	Re: Jury finds Randy Taylor guilty of Alexis Murphy's murder	WTVR.com

You will still need to rewrite all those chapters in your voice. That, by definition, is new material. Those chapters as currently written belong to Dan Baldwin and Kelly Snyder and are part of the Find Me II book. You can't just take them and dump them into another book. That won't work.

We need to wrap this book and get it out there now. You can draft your version and roll with that.

----- Original Message -----
From: kelly snyder
To: Dan
Sent: Monday, April 13, 2015 10:58 AM
Subject: Re: Jury finds Randy Taylor guilty of Alexis Murphy's murder | WTVR.com

The chapters that I would want in the separate book are also some of the chapters that you are referring to also .. I don't know which of those chapters (cases) I would select, so that is what I am trying to sort out...

It's not a different book, it is the same book only in my way of doing it with "some" of the same cases..... that is what I am trying to deal with...

I should know more by 23rd or 24th....

On Apr 13, 2015, at 8:05 AM, Dan Baldwin <baldco@msn.com> wrote:

I'll hold off until the end of the month on cleaning up the new chapters.

After a lot of thinking on this, I don't see how you can sort out what appears
to be unsortable. FIND ME II is done and essentially ready to go. The book she
wants you to write is entirely different book and you can't morph this one
into that one for lots of sound reasons.

Appendix 29

Dan Baldwin

From:	"Dan Baldwin" <baldco@msn.com>
To:	"kelly snyder" <kilomonster1@gmail.com>
Sent:	Friday, May 8, 2015 3:06 PM
Subject:	Re: Find Me Also

Have fun.

If the contract is for our book, I need to see a copy of it.

If it's for the Kelly book, no need.
I'll wrap the gramma/spelling check on the new chapters this weekend.

Dan

> ----- Original Message -----
> **From:** kelly snyder
> **To:** Dan
> **Sent:** Friday, May 8, 2015 2:43 PM
> **Subject:** Re: Find Me Also
>
> Leaving in two hours for Japan, so can't get to anything right now... she sent me a contract, but Denise and or TV - entertainment attorney have it... waiting for response...
>
> I am back on the 18th and then we can talk..
>
> KS
>
> > On May 6, 2015, at 6:23 AM, Dan Baldwin <baldco@msn.com> wrote:
> >
> > Dan Baldwin
> > 480-807-9682
> > baldco@msn.com
> > www.fourknightspress.com www.danbaldwin.biz
> > My Political/Crime thriller Sparky and the King is available in ebook and paperback at: https://www.smashwords.com/books/view/490723
> >
> >
> > Kelly,
> >
> > FYI - I'm over the flu finally and have caught up with my writing projects.
> >
> > I'll be working on our book this week and will finish the grammar/spelling/style
> > review of the new chapters. All we will need is your input on those chapters.
> >
> > We can do that in an interview like last time or even on the phone - I know
> > you're covered up.

Appendix 30

Dan Baldwin

From: "kelly snyder" <kilomonster1@gmail.com>
To: "Dan Baldwin" <baldco1@msn.com>
Sent: Wednesday, June 17, 2015 10:29 AM
Subject: Fwd:

Begin forwarded message:

From: "Dan Baldwin" <baldco@msn.com>
Date: June 17, 2015 at 6:14:32 AM MST
To: "Kelly Snyder" <kilomonster1@gmail.com>

Kelly,

1. What happened w/the Cynthia deal? It took Denise and Cynthia about two weeks before they talked and supposedly Cynthia is rewriting the contract offer to "allow" for Denise's concerns to be corrected because of my contract with her. So.... waiting for the updated contract to arrive..!!..??
   I got a contact with a highly-touted agent last night and I'll be following up today. I'd like to mention Find Me - The Casebook.

2. What's your mailing address? I have a copy of The Practical Pendulum with you name on it. 2770 E. Buena Vista Dr Chandler 85249

3. I can't make the Sept. 13 meeting. I'll be on a mini book tour back in Louisiana. OK..

Dan'l

Appendix 31

May 16, 2016

Mr. Kelly Snyder
2770 E. Buena Vista Drive
Chandler, AZ 85249

Ms. Sunny Dawn Johnson
4634 Redfield Road
Glendale, AZ 85306

Mr. Dave Campbell
THE ASTROLOGY STORE
5735 West Glendale Ave.
Glendale, AZ 85301

Board of Directors-Find Me
Via Email only:
Kilcmonster1@gmail.com
sundowj@cox.net
theastrologystore@gmail.com
jwdenboer@yahoo.com
qualitmater@seanet.com
rega.comcto@gmail.com

RE: Mr. Dan Baldwin

Ladies and Gentlemen:

I am in receipt of Mr. Snyder's email letter regarding Mr. Baldwin's request to rescind his termination from your records and thus reinstating him onto the Board of Directors of Find Me. Immediately upon the reinstatement, Mr. Baldwin is prepared to submit the enclosed resignation. The Board can then accept the resignation.

Mr. Baldwin, at my suggestion, believes that the Board can correct the minutes by stating "Dan Baldwin was not in violation of the Find Me code of ethics and has been reinstated as a member in good standing to the Board of Directors." In this way, the record is clear, concise and correct.

459 N. Granada Avenue
Tucson, Arizona 85701   520.622.4622 (Ph)
tom@mediationoftucson.com   520.882.9861 (Fax)

Continued on next page

Page 2
Letter Dated 5/16/2016
Baldwin/Find Me

So that everyone is on board, Mr. Baldwin and the Board of Directors can agree as follows:

1. Find Me will reinstate Mr. Baldwin as a member and Board Member in good standing;

2. The Board of Directors' action reinstating Mr. Baldwin will be entered into the official minutes;

3. Mr. Baldwin will execute and tender his resignation in writing.

4. Each member of Find Me will be notified of Mr. Baldwin's reinstatement in good standing in a message separate from the minutes;

5. The Board of Directors of Arizona Search Track and Rescue (AZ-STAR) will be notified both of the reinstatement and subsequent resignation;

6. Denise Goodwin Pace of Looking Productions will be notified both of the reinstatement and subsequent resignation;

7. Maria Crimi Speth of Jaburg-Wilkes Attorneys at Law will be notified both of the reinstatement and subsequent resignation; and

8. Mr. Baldwin will not discuss or make any disparaging remarks about the organization and the organization will act likewise toward him.

I have enclosed an unsigned copy of the purposed resignation and agreement from Mr. Baldwin. I have asked him to execute it and return it to me so that I in turn can forward it to each of you upon completion of this transaction.

I also want to take this opportunity to thank Mr. Baldwin and each of you for resolving this issue using alternative dispute resolution.

So that we can have this completed and finalized by the end of this month, may I suggest that you do what is necessary in order to re-instate Mr. Baldwin and correct the record and Mr. Baldwin, you execute the letter of resignation and return it to me so I can forward it to the Find Me organization. I would like to

Continued on next page

115

Page 3
Letter Dated 5/16/2016
Baldwin/Find Me

have everything in hand no later than Friday May 27, 2016. So that this transaction is completed by Tuesday May 31, 2016.

If any individual or entity has a question, please let me know.

Thank you.

Sincerely,

Thomas T. Tilton
Mediation of Tucson

TTT/mm
cc: Mr. Dan Baldwin
Enclosure

Appendix 32

July 9, 2015

Kelly,

Your recent telephone conversations and e-mails have astounded me. I am heartsick that you have so misconstrued at this late date the development of our book project, *Find Me II – The Casebook*. I would have responded to your last two e-mails more quickly, but I really was shaken by your words and I also wanted to double check my records to verify some of the facts stated below. Clearly, your memory and your facts as stated are seriously flawed. To set the record straight here is what is and what was.

What Is.

When you abandoned our project earlier this year (for example, not responding to repeated requests for your input) to pursue a contract for your own book with the agent Cynthia Cannell, you left me with the responsibility of finishing the project and that is what I have done.

Find Me II – The Casebook is now in e-mail and paperback formats and will be available no later than early next week (possibly by this weekend) through Amazon (Kindle), Smashwords, Barnes & Noble, CreateSpace and other distributors. As I said, I write to publish, not to sit on a project and not to give it away.

I e-mailed last month that I was moving on to complete the project. You used the term "takeover" in your most recent e-mail. That is an inaccurate and unfortunate term. I have simply finished a project we started - just as I said I would do. Again, (1) your abandonment of the project, (2) your seeking of your own project on the same subject, and (3) the overlong length of time involved in this project were contributing factors to wrapping this up at this time.

What was.

Your statement that our project began in 2011 or 2012 with me agreeing to help write your book in your voice is in error.

I approached you in 2009 about co-writing a book on Find Me cases and you accepted.

This was always a co-author project. There was no mention of this being "your" book or a "Kelly Snyder" book.

The project isn't and has never been a Find Me organization project. It's a Dan Baldwin and Kelly Snyder project.

As you know, every title page from day one has been slugged "Dan Baldwin and Kelly Snyder."

There was no discussion and certainly no decision to write the casebook in your voice. This was never a ghostwriting project.

In 2009 we discussed the writing style to be used and agreed that I would write in the standard style used on most of my ghostwriting projects for business books and that was used in the as-told-to book I wrote on Find Me with some of our original group.

(more)

Continued on next page

Page Two of Two

In your e-mail (7/6/15) you mentioned a meeting where we discussed writing a book in your voice and that I offered to help you with it. I have absolutely no recollection of such a meeting or any such discussion. Even assuming faulty memory on my part, a book in your voice discussed at that time was clearly a separate book (a term you used in an e-mail to me on the subject) and not *Find Me II – The Casebook*.

(I offered to help you write a book in your voice, but that offer was made this year and in direct reference to the book you're working on with Cynthia. That offer stands.)

The first time the theme of writing in your voice came up was in mid-April this year when you e-mailed me that Cynthia wanted you to do your own book in your own voice.

That's the timeframe in which you abandoned our project and started seeking your own. I offered my support for your new project, but noted that you could not take our project and put your name on it or modify it for that purpose. The information in *Find Me II* is not proprietary, but the form in which it is presented is. You are free to write your own version in your own words.

I use the term abandon accurately. I have for months requested your input on the newest chapters – those suggested by Joni. You have never responded despite my repeated requests.

I asked if you wanted to update your photo or bio for the back cover, but, again, you did not respond.

I mentioned an estimate for the hard costs of producing the book and splitting them. Again, there was no response. (Those costs are minimal and within the range I mentioned to you.)

When I mentioned the deal I negotiated for the front cover photo and front cover design (we got both for gratis from a national award winning graphic designer), you made no comment, not even a request to see the design.

Last month I e-mailed you that I was pushing ahead with completion of the project and that is what I have done. Of course, our 50/50 profit split agreement stands.

I am surprised and saddened by your recent abandonment of a book we have worked on for so long, but I do wish you the best of luck with your other book.

The bottom line in all of this is that *Find Me II – The Casebook* is, after six years of labor, finally in the marketplace. I have faith that it will do well.

Dan

Appendix 33

Note that in reference to the book Snyder writes "It's yours to keep..." followed by a censorship demand.

Dan Baldwin

From:	"Dan Baldwin" <baldco@centurylink.net>
To:	<baldco@msn.com>
Sent:	Monday, July 27, 2015 12:57 PM
Subject:	Fwd: Co-Founder reverence

From: "kelly snyder" <kilomonster1@gmail.com>
To: "Dan Baldwin" <baldco@centurylink.net>
Sent: Friday, July 17, 2015 11:52:41 AM
Subject: Fwd: Co-Founder reverence

Begin forwarded message:

From: Dan Baldwin <baldco@centurylink.net>
Subject: Re: Co-Founder reverence
Date: July 17, 2015 at 9:42:36 AM MST
To: kelly snyder <kilomonster1@gmail.com>, sunnydawn@cox.net, theastrologystore@gmail.com, jwdenboer@yahoo.com, quailhunter@seanet.com, peg.rometo@gmail.com, baldco@msn.com

Kelly,
I continue in response to comments coming my way.

The e-mail you sent to me and the board yesterday addressed my "lack of truthfulness." In that e-mail you stated unambiguously "I have personally "never" heard you use the that term co-founder in my presence." Your e-mail to me of July 8, 2015 says just the opposite. "For the record I have only heard you make that reference in recent months." I wanted the board to be aware of this contradiction. That reference is from NYC eventâ€¦ how much more clearer can I make this..??

As to the book (working title Find Me Two): As promised I will forward a clarification to the board today.

Also, your e-mail to me July 14, 2015 states that "I do not want any part or portion of the book..." I take you at your word on that. Itâ€™s yours to keep, just make sure there are NO references that I have anything to do with it and that NONE of my

Continued on next page

comments are in the bookâ€¦. Find Me name cannot be made reference to either or that this is sanctioned by Find Me. My attorney will be sending you a confirmation of all of this. so that there are NO misunderstandings...

As always, I am available to any board member to answer any questions Final emailâ€¦ it is now in the hands of attorneys and youâ€¦..
about this matter.

Dan

From: "kelly snyder" <kilomonster1@gmail.com>
To: "Dan Baldwin" <baldco@centurylink.net>
Sent: Friday, July 17, 2015 8:35:00 AM
Subject: Re: Co-Founder reverence

It refers to the NYC eventâ€¦. why keep up this diatribe when it is obvious you are reaching for anything to take the focus off of youâ€¦.

We will now wait to see what your move is about the bookâ€¦.

On Jul 16, 2015, at 2:36 PM, Dan Baldwin <baldco@centurylink.net> wrote:

Kelly,

Regarding truthfulness:

Your statement to the board of directors of Find Me about you never hearing me use the term "co-founder"
in your presence is, as you know, false.

This is the line cut directly from your e-mail:

Appendix 34

3200 N. CENTRAL AVENUE, 20TH FLOOR, PHOENIX, AZ 85012

jaburgwilk.com

Maria Crimi Speth

mcs@jaburgwilk.com
602.248.1089 – Direct Phone
602.248.0522 – Main Fax

July 29, 2015

Via E-Mail: baldco1@msn.com
                baldco@msn.com
                baldco@centurylink.net

and U. S. Mail

Gary J. Jaburg
Lawrence E. Wilk
Roger L. Cohen
Mitchell Reichman
Beth S. Cohn
Kraig J. Marton
Ronald M. Horwitz
Maria Crimi Speth
Neal H. Bookspan
Kathi M. Sandweiss
Marvyn T. Braude
Lauren L. Garner
Michelle C. Lombino
Janessa E. Koenig
Mark D. Bogard
David N. Farren
David L. Allen
Laurence B. Hirsch
Jennifer R. Erickson
Nathan D. Meyer
Jason B. Castle
Douglas O. Guffey
C. Cole Crabtree
Erick S. Durlach
Thomas S. Moring
Matthew Y. Anderson
Laura A. Rogal
Amy M. Horwitz
Nichole H. Wilk
Jeffrey A. Silence
Shawdy Banihashemi
Aaron K. Haar

Dan Baldwin
6311 E. Regina St.
Mesa, AZ 85215

   Re: *Copyright Infringement -- Find Me*

Dear Mr. Baldwin:

   This firm represents Kelly Snyder and Find Me, Inc. in connection with the protection and enforcement of their intellectual property rights. I understand that you and Mr. Snyder had been working together over the past three-and-a-half years to co-author a book about the Find Me group. I also understand that the two of you ultimately parted ways. You have since claimed that you "copyrighted" the book, including Mr. Snyder's portion, and that you intend to move forward with publishing the book on your own. I also understand that you have previously incorrectly represented yourself as a co-founder of Find Me.

   The purpose of this letter is two-fold: (1) to demand that you not use Mr. Snyder's copyright-protected work; and (2) to demand that you immediately cease using the trademark FIND ME in any way that suggests sponsorship, endorsement, or affiliation with you or your work.

Mr. Snyder's Writings

   Regardless of any action you may have taken to register the copyright in the planned book, Mr. Snyder retains the copyrights in the material he created/authored. Copyrights in a given work automatically vest in the author of the work. *See* 17 U.S.C. § 201(a). Mr. Snyder independently authored 17 of the chapters in the draft of the book. Mr. Snyder also created various audio recordings in connection with the book, for which he similarly retains copyrights. Mr. Snyder's copyrights in these works are exclusive rights under the Copyright Act, 17 U.S.C. § 106.

Continued on next page

JABURG|WILK
Attorneys at Law
Dan Baldwin
July 29, 2015
Page 2

For you to have any claim to these chapters and audio recordings, Mr. Snyder would have had to affirmatively assign his rights in the works to you. An assignment of copyright must be in writing pursuant to 17 U.S.C. § 204(a) and must be clear and unequivocal. *The Weinstein Company v. Smokewood Entertainment Group, LLC*, 664 F. Supp. 2d 332, 340 (S.D.N.Y. 2009). Indeed, the very purpose of §204(a) is that it "ensures that the creator of a work will not give away his copyright inadvertently and forces a party who wants to use the copyrighted work to negotiate with the creator to determine precisely what rights are being transferred and at what price." *Effects Assoc., Inc. v. Cohen*, 908 F.2d 555, 557 (9th Cir.1990); *see Konigsberg Int'l, Inc.*, 16 F.3d 355, 357 (9th Cir. 1994). Moreover, "§ 204(a)'s writing requirement not only protects authors from fraudulent claims, but also enhances predictability and certainty of ownership—Congress's paramount goal when it revised the Act in 1976." *Id.* (internal citations omitted); *see also Schiller & Schmidt, Inc. v. Nordisco Corp.*, 969 F.2d 410, 412 (7th Cir. 1992) (holding that [17 U.S.C.] § 101's requirements of a written statement for copyright ownership of works for hire "is not merely a statute of frauds"; it is also intended "to make the ownership of property rights in intellectual property clear and definite, so that such property will be readily marketable"). Since Mr. Snyder has not executed any such assignment, it is undisputed that he retains exclusive ownership of the copyrights in the portions of the book that he wrote.

Moreover, it is copyright infringement to copy a work in its entirety, or to copy constituent elements of the work that are original. *Feist Publications,Inc. v. Rural Telephone Service Co., Inc.*, 499 U.S. 340, 361, 111 S.Ct. 1282, 113 L.Ed.2d 358 (1991). Thus, you may not use Mr. Snyder's authored works even if you make changes or revisions to it. To the extent you take and use any of that work, or adopt that work in similar form, you will be liable for copyright infringement. Such action would constitute a willful infringement of my client's copyrights, which would entitle Mr. Snyder to recover the damages and obtain injunctive relief. *See* 17 U.S.C. § 504–505.

Moreover, the Copyright Act makes it a federal crime to willfully infringe ones copyrights for commercial advantage or private financial gain. 17 U.S.C. § 506(a). Making a false representation of a material fact—such as claims of ownership—in a copyright registration also constitutes a federal crime. *See id.* § 506(e). Therefore, you are advised that any actions you take, or have taken, to use or register my client's works will subject you to both civil and criminal liability.

The FIND ME Trademark

The Find Me organization maintains exclusive right to use the trademark FIND ME in connection with missing persons investigations. This mark has been used in commerce continually since 2003. The mark is registered with the United States Patent and Trademark Office under Registration No. 4427655.

The "core element" of trademark infringement law is whether an alleged trademark infringer's use of a mark creates a likelihood of confusion as to who is behind the product. *See Brother Records, Inc. v. Jardine*, 318 F.3d 900, 908 (9th Cir. 2003). Any false assertion or implication of sponsorship, endorsement, or affiliation constitutes trademark infringement. *See Mattel, Inc. v. Walking Mountain Productions*, 353 F.3d 792, 806–807, 69 U.S.P.Q.2d 1257 (9th Cir. 2003) ("Generally, to assess whether a defendant has infringed on a plaintiff's trademark, we apply a 'likelihood of confusion' test that asks whether use of the plaintiff's trademark by the defendant is 'likely to cause confusion or to cause

Continued on next page

JABURG|WILK
Attorneys at Law
Dan Baldwin
July 29, 2015
Page 3

mistake, or to deceive as to the affiliation, connection, or association' of the two products."). Given that any book you publish will directly compete with any book actually sanctioned by Find Me, the likelihood of confusion is quite high. *See AMF Inc. v. Sleekcraft Boats*, 599 F.2d 341, 348 (9th Cir. 1979) ("When the goods produced by the alleged infringer compete for sales with those of the trademark owner, infringement usually will be found if the marks are sufficiently similar that confusion can be expected."). Federal statutes provide for civil remedies for infringement of a trademark, including damages, costs, and attorney fees. 15 U.S.C. § 1114.

Thus, to the extent you choose to move forward with publishing your original writings, you may not use the trademark FIND ME in any way that suggests sponsorship, endorsement, or affiliation with you or with your work. You also may not use Mr. Snyder's name or imply any sponsorship, endorsement, or affiliation with Mr. Snyder. And you may not falsely state or imply that you are a co-founder of Find Me. Moreover, I note that you are currently subject to an agreement with Denise Goodwin Pace that restricts your ability to write about Mr. Snyder without prior written approval. Contract damages may also be available to Ms. Pace if you violate that agreement.

Conclusion

In conclusion, you must refrain from using or registering any of Mr. Snyder's work. To the extent you have already submitted any portion of Mr. Snyder's work for federal copyright registration, you must immediately withdraw the application from consideration. You must also immediately cease using the mark FIND ME in any way that suggests sponsorship, endorsement, or affiliation with you or your work. You also may not use Mr. Snyder's name or imply any sponsorship, endorsement, or affiliation with Mr. Snyder. And you may not falsely state or imply that you are a co-founder of Find Me. Please respond to this letter in writing no later than August 7, 2015 to confirm you will comply with these demands.

Sincerely,

JABURG & WILK, P.C.

Maria Crimi Speth

MCS:akh

Appendix 35

September 8, 2015

SENT VIA U.S. MAIL &
EMAIL:mcs@jburgwilk.com
Maria Crimi Speth, Esq.
Jaburg/Wilk
3200 No. Central Ave., #20 Floor
Phoenix, AZ 85021

      RE: Dan Baldwin and Kelly Snyder: "FIND ME"

Dear Ms. Speth:

By way of introduction, my name is Thomas Tilton and I am a mediator with Mediation of Tucson.

I have met with Mr. Dan Baldwin, examined the documentation that he brought in regarding his association with Mr. Kelly Snyder and reviewed your letter of July 29, 2015.

Mr. Baldwin is interested in resolving the situation described in your July 29th letter. He is amenable to meeting with you and Mr. Snyder in an attempt to resolve any perceived issue involving the "FIND ME" trademarks, writings, etc.

I am assured by Mr. Baldwin that he has no intention of using Mr. Snyder's copy write-protected work and that he would certainly not use the trademark "FIND ME" in any manner that would suggest Mr. Snyder's sponsorship, endorsement or affiliation with Mr. Baldwin and/or his work.

Mr. Baldwin relates that while they were attempting to work on a book together, Mr. Baldwin authored the final draft of the entire book. Clearly, the writing style indicates that it was written by one or two people. In addition, when you compare the book in question to Mr. Baldwin's other 60+ books, you can see that they are similar in content, style, organization, spelling and grammar.

While Mr. Baldwin acknowledges that Mr. Snyder wrote some of the content, Mr. Baldwin is only using interviews or other information obtained by him and not by any other individual, i.e. Mr. Snyder. Mr. Baldwin has proof of this and can provide all documents relevant thereto.

459 N. Granada Avenue
Tucson, Arizona 85701   520.622.4622

Continued on next page

Page -2-
Maria Crimi Speth, Esq.
September 8, 2015

I suggested that if there is an issue as to which individual may have written a particular chapter that both he and Mr. Snyder provide their work product, i.e. notes, interviews, writings, etc.

It does not appear that there has been any real or imagined infringement by Mr. Baldwin toward any other individual in general and Mr. Snyder, in particular. The writing appears to be Mr. Baldwin's own personal style.

I believe the above would be a fair and equitable way to provide "proof of product."

Mr. Baldwin also indicated that Mr. Snyder knew about the "co-founder" issue as early as 2009, and in fact, Mr. Baldwin was shown on the jacket cover as a co-founder of "FIND ME." Apparently, it was also shown on the "FIND ME" website that was available to not only Mr. Baldwin and Mr. Snyder, but to anyone going to the website. I believe Mr. Baldwin has already removed the title "co-founder" and will continue to do so.

I am assured that the book at issue was never intended to be a "FIND ME" organizational publication. There was no logo for "FIND ME" in the book, it was not authorized by the organization and I do not believe there was any intent by anyone to suggest a connection. I don't believe there has been any confusion or misunderstanding regarding the book and the "FIND ME" organization.

Mr. Baldwin wanted me to assure you and Mr. Snyder that Mr. Snyder would not be referred to as a co-author, author, or in any other manner in the book. While Mr. Snyder can be removed as having any interest or authorship to the publication, Mr. Baldwin's interviews and writings will be included within the publication.

There will be no confusion between the originally proposed "FIND ME" book and whatever Mr. Baldwin decides to name his publication.

I have been told by Mr. Baldwin that he and Mr. Snyder had been working on this project since 2009. It is not a new project.

Mr. Baldwin is certainly desirous of avoiding confrontation and litigation and yet, he is of the strong belief and opinion that he has the right to go forward on this, his sole and separate project. Please be assured as indicated above, that Mr. Baldwin will remove any reference to Mr. Snyder, "FIND ME," and will remove any work product that may have been contributed by Mr. Snyder.

Continued on next page

Page -3-
Maria Crimi Speth, Esq.
September 8, 2015

Once again, if Mr. Snyder and you would like to meet with Mr. Baldwin personally, he is happy to do so.

I look forward to hearing from you. I am also happy to help resolve this matter in any way possible.

Thank you.

Sincerely,

Thomas T. Tilton
Mediation of Tucson

TTT/bb

cc: Mr. Dan Baldwin

Appendix 36

Find Me, Too

(Working Title)

© Dan Baldwin/Kelly Snyder 2009

Appendix 37

ABOUT THE AUTHORS

Dan Baldwin is an inaugural member of FIND ME, a volunteer group of psychics, retired and active law enforcement personnel, legal and investigative experts, and search and rescue teams committed to finding missing persons and solving crimes. He often participates in "ground pounding" with the group's sister organization, Arizona Search, Track and Rescue (AZ-STAR).

He is the author, co-author or ghostwriter of more than 50 books on business. He is the author of the Caldera series of westerns, *Trapp Canyon*, a western, the mysteries *Desecration, Heresy* and *Vengeance*, and the thriller *Sparky and the King*. He is the winner of numerous local, regional, and national awards for writing and directing film and video projects. He earned an Honorable Mention from the Society of Southwestern Authors writing competition for his short story *Flat Busted* and earned a Finalist designation from the National Indie Excellence Awards for *Trapp Canyon* and for *Caldera III – A Man of Blood*. Baldwin is a resident of Phoenix-Mesa, Arizona.

Continued on next page

When **Kelly Snyder** saw a need for aggressive efforts to find missing persons he founded FIND ME to support the efforts of law enforcement and to provide closure to families and individuals affected by the loss of a friend or member of the family. He is a career law enforcement officer with experience in the U.S. Customs Service and the Drug Enforcement Administration.

A Four Knights Press Publication
Copyright © 2015 by Dan Baldwin and Jerry "Kelly" Snyder

* * * * *

Continued on next page

Disclaimer

FIND ME II: The Casebook is not an approved instructional text for law enforcement, search and rescue activities, or for those who seek to assist in those operations This book is for entertainment purposes only, and nothing in it should be construed as encouragement to interfere in official police business or operations, or to intrude upon the privacy of individuals or families. The narrative and advice contained herein reflect solely the opinions, experiences and best knowledge of the authors, participants, and members of the Find Me organization, as told to Mr. Baldwin. Some names have been changed to protect the privacy of those involved.

* * * * *

Front cover design by Gary Cascio. LateNite Grafix, Inc.
Front cover photo © 2015 Gary Cascio.LateNite Grafix, In
Formatting by Debora Lewis arenapublishing.org

Appendix 38

Dan Baldwin

From: "Dan Baldwin" <baldco@msn.com>
To: "Kelly Snyder" <kilomonster@centurylink.net>
Sent: Saturday, June 27, 2015 7:16 AM
Subject: Fw:

https://flic.kr/p/ucbXxr

Photo selected for the Find Me II - Casebook.

The photographer has granted us full rights to use it
for the cover and any promotion directly related to
the book - gratis.

He'll get cover credit of course.

The back cover and spine from the first book will
serve for this one.

My friend from Santa Fe is designing the cover. He
is a national award winning graphic designer. He's
also agreed to work gratis - cover credit is all
he wants.

I'll send the manuscript in for formating (e-book
and paperback) in one week. If you can, get me
you comments on the new chapters.

Dan'l

Appendix 39

Find Me II – The Casebook was a push of a button away from distribution. Does this look like I have copyrighted the work under my own name as the officers and board of directors claimed?

Appendix 40

Note that the way at least three board members have been removed follows a pattern that violates the group's (IRS) 501c3 bylaws. Note also the term "unanimous." Just as a point of order, you can't have a unanimous vote if one of the members is excluded from the meeting.

Dan Baldwin

From:	"Sunny Dawn Johnston" <sdj@sunnydawnjohnston.com>
To:	"Dan Baldwin" <baldco@msn.com>
Cc:	"Kelly Snyder" <kilomonster1@gmail.com>
Sent:	Monday, March 7, 2016 6:29 PM
Subject:	response to your request

Mr. Baldwin,

The process created by the Find ME Board, which you were a member of since 2011 is that all volunteers agree to the code of ethics. You, along with all members of the board agreed that all matters/violations would be decided upon by the board of directors on a per individual basis. The board would then decide and vote on the appropriate action to be taken. You have been involved in at least two of those personnel actions during your tenure as a board member. The same process was used in your case. The vote to remove you from the board was unanimous. Your follow up comments to the board on your removal were read and the decision to remove you was confirmed.

The board has once again reviewed your most recent correspondence and their decision remains final. You will not be reinstated.

Sincerely,

The Find Me Group Board of Directors

Appendix 41

Find Me II – The Casebook was in the distributors' catalog needing only my activation for distribution. Again, why the officers and board of directors claimed I had planned on copyrighting the book under my own name is contradicted by a stack of documentation in their possession or available to them.

Find Me II – The Casebook
Authored by Dan Baldwin, Authored with Kelly Snyder

Continued on next page

List Price: **$14.99**
6" x 9" (15.24 x 22.86 cm)
Black & White on White paper
220 pages
ISBN-13:   **978-1515062523**   (CreateSpace-Assigned)   ISBN-10: 151506252X
BISAC: **Body, Mind & Spirit / Spiritualism / General**

FIND ME – a wild dream in the mind of a practical man – is an international organization respected by law enforcement agencies throughout the world and a refuge for frightened and heart-broken families and friends of missing persons, an effective instrument of law enforcement feared by criminals and predators, and a welcoming place where common folks with uncommon gifts can make significant contributions to bettering the world. FIND ME II – The Casebook is primarily a book about some of the cases resulting from the realization of that vision. You will read about our work...

Appendix 42

The reasonable suggestion that we allow an independent judge to settle the disagreements in a legally binding environment went unanswered.

November 25, 2015

SENT VIA U.S. MAIL &
EMAIL:mcs@jaburgwilk.com
Maria Crimi Speth, Esq.
Jaburg/Wilk
3200 No. Central Ave., #20 Floor
Phoenix, AZ 85021

RE: Dan Baldwin and Kelly Snyder: "FIND ME"

Dear Ms. Speth:

I have spoken to Dan Baldwin again since forwarding my email to you dated November 2, 2015. You responded on November 3, 2015, indicating that Mr. Snyder wasn't able to review the entire manuscript and respond by November 9th.

While Mr. Baldwin understood the need for some time to review the materials, and has delayed his publication date, he would now like to move forward.

Mr. Baldwin reminded me that there are a number of emails in which Mr. Snyder recognized Mr. Baldwin's right to publish, provided that he (Mr. Snyder) was not associated with the book as an author. As you know, Mr. Baldwin has agreed to all legal and reasonable requests and wants to move forward.

Mr. Baldwin also has indicated to me that the current version of the manuscript now in Mr. Snyder's hands is essentially the same as the manuscript he has had in his possession all year—the only difference being, at Mr. Snyder's request, references to him (Mr. Snyder) as an author or co-author, have been removed.

Mr. Baldwin is very concerned that Mr. Snyder may have made inaccurate and/or false statements to you and your law firm, but has hinted that he may disseminate the correspondence regarding the copyright issue to other entities— any or all which have damaged Mr. Baldwin's reputation and which has the potential to have a negative impact on his potential earning ability. If, in fact, Mr. Snyder follows through with this type of unsubstantiated and potentially misleading threat, Mr. Baldwin will have no alternative but to litigate. He prefers not to do so.

459 N. Granada Avenue
Tucson, Arizona 85701   520 622 4622 (Ph)

Continued on next page

Page -2-
Maria Crimi Speth, Esq.
November 25, 2015

Mr. Baldwin prefers the appointment of an independent third party to act as editor/judge/arbitrator to determine authorship. To aid in that evaluation, the arbitrator should receive manuscripts and other material to assist him/her in determining whether the book is written as "two voices" or a single voice. Each party would also be required to authenticate those chapters that they have claimed to have written.

I suggested to Mr. Baldwin that he and Mr. Snyder could present work samples from some of the published works that each has authored or co-authored, for comparison of the manuscript of this recent work.

Mr. Baldwin shared that Mr. Snyder also claims copyrights to tapes he (Mr. Snyder) claims to have provided for this work. Mr. Baldwin has shared that there have never been any tapes produced and that two interviews were conducted by Mr. Baldwin from Mr. Snyder for the sole purpose of recording raw data for use in the manuscript. These two interviews apparently were done by Mr. Baldwin using his personal hand held digital recorder.

I really think that it is time to move forward and conclude this matter between these two gentlemen. If Mr. Snyder has no interest in arbitrating/mediating the matter, then Mr. Baldwin is moving forward with the book. You originally asked Mr. Baldwin to delay his proposed publication date until the beginning of December. He has done so.

Mr. Baldwin is prepared to move forward with his publication on December 2, 2015.

Sincerely,

Thomas T. Tilton
Mediation of Tucson

TTT/bb

cc: Mr. Dan Baldwin

Appendix 43

CenturyLink Webmail   **baldco@centurylink.net**

Re: Find Me II

From : Dan Baldwin <baldco@centurylink.net>   Tue, Jun 23, 2015 06:04 PM

Subject : Re: Find Me II

To : kelly snyder <kilomonster1@gmail.com>

I'm working on a new cover now. The old cover w/new title is the backup.

As described, I don't think the other issue is resolvable. We can't knife Denise et al in the back and give away rights that can't be given away.

Indie publication makes incredibly more sense than agent/traditional publication in terms of rights, payment, timeframe, and flexibility.

I'll push ahead on that end and have matters ready to hit "send" pretty soon.

Good luck w/the agent, but watch your back.

Dan

From: "kelly snyder" <kilomonster1@gmail.com>

To: "Dan Baldwin" <baldco@centurylink.net>

Sent: Tuesday, June 23, 2015 1:53:33 PM

Subject: Re: Find Me II

Ok... stand by ... still attempting to resolve the other issue..!!

> On Jun 23, 2015, at 8:49 AM, Dan Baldwin <baldco@centurylink.net> wrote:

Kelly,

Regarding your comments on the new chapters in Find Me II:

I can't put in what you won't provide. Please get those to me or the book will have to be published as is. It will be better with your comments.

Appendix 44

Dan Baldwin

From: "Dan Baldwin" <baldco@msn.com>
To: "Kelly Snyder" <kilomonster@centurylink.net>
Sent: Saturday, June 27, 2015 7:16 AM
Subject: Fw:

https://flic.kr/p/ucbXxr

Photo selected for the Find Me II - Casebook.

The photographer has granted us full rights to use it for the cover and any promotion directly related to the book - gratis.

He'll get cover credit of course.

The back cover and spine from the first book will serve for this one.

My friend from Santa Fe is designing the cover. He is a national award winning graphic designer. He's also agreed to work gratis - cover credit is all he wants.

I'll send the manuscript in for formating (e-book and paperback) in one week. If you can, get me you comments on the new chapters.

Dan'l

Appendix 45

From: tom@mediationoftucson.com [mailto:tom@mediationoftucson.com]
Sent: Monday, November 02, 2015 9:26 AM
To: Maria Crimi Speth
Cc: baldco@msn.com
Subject: Dan Baldwin/Kelly Snyder: Manuscript

Dear Ms. Speth:

Thank you for your email note of 10/08/15 regarding Mssrs. Baldwin and Snyder.

Mr. Baldwin spoke to me again regarding a conclusion, and authorized me to communicate with you. He also authorized you and Mr. Snyder seeing the final manuscript prior to publication. It is attached. Mr. Baldwin specifically indicated, however, that nothing is to be changed, altered, or amended to his writing. It is being included with the understanding by Mr. Snyder and any of his agents that the entire content of this book is the sole property of Mr. Baldwin.

Continued on next page

Apparently, Mr. Baldwin presented this manuscript to Ms. Cynthia Cannell in February, 2015. A copy of this correspondence and manuscript was copied to Mr. Snyder on the same date. He indicates that he started this work in 2009.

New chapters to the book were added in June, 2015. Mr. Baldwin advised me that he had emailed Mr. Snyder throughout early 2015 and into the summer, about the book and its progress. Per Mr. Baldwin, he made repeated efforts to get Mr. Snyder to comment on the book during that time period, but for whatever reason, was not able to do so.

As you can see, and pursuant to Mr. Snyder's request, Mr. Baldwin has removed his name and copy write from the book. In addition, Mr. Baldwin pulled Mr. Snyder's name and biography from any mention in the book. Additionally, Mr. Baldwin removed Mr. Snyder's chapter entitled "The Looking Forward" chapter. Also, the Kristi Smith chapter has been removed.

Mr. Baldwin shares with me that Mr. Snyder is still in the book and is credited as a source, but has been removed and will not be quoted or cited as a co-author.

In an effort to ensure that Mr. Snyder's requests were met, I have reviewed the book and see no reference to Mr. Snyder as an author, co-author, contributor, copy write co-owner, or in any other capacity. It appears to me that Mr. Snyder has been fully removed from having any relationship in any capacity to this manuscript.

Mr. Baldwin is desirous of getting this issue finalized between himself and Mr. Snyder. To that end, Mr. Baldwin indicates that he intends to publish his work immediately after the 9th of November, 2015.

I am happy to be of assistance in this matter.

Sincerely,

Thomas T. Tilton

Mediation of Tucson

Continued on next page

Dan Baldwin

From:	"Maria Crimi Speth" <mcs@jaburgwilk.com>
To:	<tom@mediationoftucson.com>
Cc:	<baldco@msn.com>
Sent:	Tuesday, November 3, 2015 6:28 PM
Attach:	image001.png; image003.jpg
Subject:	RE: Dan Baldwin/Kelly Snyder: Manuscript

Mr. Tilton:

My client is not able to review the entire manuscript and respond before November 9. Based on a quick review, it does look like the manuscript contains materials written by Mr. Snyder. Mr. Baldwin should delay his proposed publication date until at least the beginning of December to give Mr. Snyder time to provide an informed and complete response.

MARIA CRIMI SPETH | Shareholder | 602.248.1089

JABURG|WILK

Attorneys at Law

From: tom@mediationoftucson.com [mailto:tom@mediationoftucson.com]
Sent: Monday, November 02, 2015 9:26 AM
To: Maria Crimi Speth
Cc: baldco@msn.com
Subject: Dan Baldwin/Kelly Snyder: Manuscript

Dear Ms. Speth:

Thank you for your email note of 10/08/15 regarding Mssrs. Baldwin and Snyder.

Mr. Baldwin spoke to me again regarding a conclusion, and authorized me to communicate with you. He also authorized you and Mr. Snyder seeing the final manuscript prior to publication. It is attached. Mr. Baldwin specifically indicated, however, that nothing is to be changed, altered, or amended to his writing. It is being included with the understanding by Mr. Snyder and any of his agents that the entire content of this book is the sole property of Mr. Baldwin.

Appendix 46

Dan Baldwin

From:	<tom@mediationoftucson.com>
To:	"'Maria Crimi Speth'" <mcs@jaburgwilk.com>
Cc:	<baldco@msn.com>
Sent:	Friday, December 18, 2015 9:24 AM
Subject:	Dan Baldwin/Kelly Snyder

Dear Ms. Speth:

I just wanted to write and let you know, since you had requested a time frame to respond, and neither Mr. Baldwin nor I had heard from you within that time frame, I have informed Mr. Baldwin I am closing my proposed mediation file. It appears that Mr. Snyder's concerns have been addressed, I have advised Mr. Baldwin of that, and he is going to go forward with the manuscript.

Mr. Baldwin assures me everything he provided to you and Mr. Snyder in early November, is accurate and truthful. Since Mr. Snyder wanted until the 1st of December to provide a response, and since it is now December 18, Mr. Baldwin is moving forward.

Thank you.

Sincerely,

Thomas T. Tilton

Mediation of Tucson

 This email has been checked for viruses by Avast antivirus software.
www.avast.com

Books by Dan Baldwin

Non-Fiction

Find Me as told to Dan Baldwin

The Practical Pendulum – Getting into the Swing of Things
by Dan Baldwin

They Are Not Yet Lost – True Stories of Psychic Detecting
by Dan Baldwin

Time Served by Dan Baldwin and Dwight and Rhonda Hull

Just the FAQs About Alcohol and Drug Abuse
(with George Sewell)

The Levine Project (with Myles and Karen Levine)

Novels

Caldera by Dan Baldwin

Caldera-A Man on Fire by Dan Baldwin

Caldera – A Man of Blood by Dan Baldwin

Trapp Canyon by Dan Baldwin

Sparky and the King-The Plot to Assassinate Elvis Presley
by Dan Baldwin

Desecration (An Ashley Hayes mystery) by Dan Baldwin

Heresy (An Ashley Hayes mystery) by Dan Baldwin

Vengeance (An Ashley Hayes Mystery) by Dan Baldwin

Bock's Canyon by Dan Baldwin (Western)

A Stalking Death by Dan Baldwin (Western)

Novellas/Short Story Collections

Vampire Bimbos on Spring Break by Dan Baldwin

Dank Summit by Dan Baldwin

Photo Books

Wildfire Stew #1

Wildfire Stew #2 – Bugs 'n Bees

Wildfire Stew #3 – More Bloomin' Arizona

Wildfire Stew #4 – The Whole Bunch

Wildflower Stew # 5 – Gila Sunrise – Stirring Things Up in New Mexico

Amazon
https://www.amazon.com/Dan-Baldwin/e/B0080Z24CO

Smashwords
https://www.smashwords.com/books/view/666742

Barnes & Noble
http://www.barnesandnoble.com/s/dan+baldwin?_requestid=1
36318

A Four Knights Press Publication
www.fourknightspress.com
Contact Dan at baldco@msn.com.

ABOUT THE AUTHOR

Dan Baldwin is the author of the westerns *Trapp Canyon, Bock's Canyon* , the *Caldera* series and *A Stalking Death*; the mysteries *Desecration, Heresy* and *Vengeance*; the thriller *Sparky and the King* and two short story collections, *Vampire Bimbos on Spring Break* and *Dank Summit and Other Stories*. He is the winner of numerous local, regional, and national awards for writing and directing film and video projects. He earned an Honorable Mention from the Society of Southwestern Authors writing competition for his short story *Flat Busted* and earned a Finalist designation from the National Indie Excellence Awards for *Trapp Canyon* and for *Caldera III – A Man of Blood* and a Finalist designation in the New Mexico-Arizona Book Awards for *Sparky and the King.* He is the ghostwriter or co-author of more than 50 books on business. Baldwin is a resident of Phoenix-Mesa, Arizona

www.ingramcontent.com/pod-product-compliance
Lightning Source LLC
Chambersburg PA
CBHW071435180526
45170CB00001B/357